ENGLISH
FOR EVERYONE

PRACTICE BOOK
LEVEL **1** BEGINNER

FREE AUDIO
website and app
www.dkefe.com

Author

Thomas Booth worked for 10 years as an English-language teacher in Poland and Russia. He now lives in England, where he works as an editor and English-language materials writer, notably of course books and vocabulary textbooks.

Course consultant

Tim Bowen has taught English and trained teachers in more than 30 countries worldwide. He is the co-author of works on pronunciation teaching and language-teaching methodology, and author of numerous books for English-language teachers. He is currently a freelance materials writer, editor, and translator. He is a member of the Chartered Institute of Linguists.

Language consultant

Professor Susan Barduhn is an experienced English-language teacher, teacher trainer, and author, who has contributed to numerous publications. In addition to directing English-language courses in at least four different continents, she has been President of the International Association of Teachers of English as a Foreign Language, and an adviser to the British Council and the US State Department. She is currently a Professor at the School for International Training in Vermont, USA.

ENGLISH
FOR EVERYONE

PRACTICE BOOK
LEVEL 1 BEGINNER

SECOND EDITION
Senior Editor Ankita Awasthi Tröger
Editor Beth Blakemore
Art Editor Amy Child
Managing Editor Carine Tracanelli
Managing Art Editor Anna Hall
Production Editor Gillian Reid
Senior Production Controller Poppy David
Senior Jacket Designer Surabhi Wadhwa-Gandhi
Jacket Design Development Manager Sophia MTT
Publisher Andrew Macintyre
Art Director Karen Self
Publishing Director Jonathan Metcalf

DK INDIA
Senior Jackets Coordinator Priyanka Sharma Saddi
DTP Designer Rakesh Kumar

FIRST EDITION
US Editors Allison Singer, Jenny Siklos
Editorial Assistants Jessica Cawthra, Sarah Edwards
Illustrators Edwood Burn, Denise Joos, Michael Parkin, Jemma Westing
Audio Producer Liz Hammond
Managing Editor Daniel Mills
Managing Art Editor Anna Hall
Project Manager Christine Stroyan
Producer, Pre-Production Luca Frassinetti
Producer Mary Slater
Jacket Designer Natalie Godwin
Jacket Editor Claire Gell
Jacket Design Development Manager Sophia MTT
Publisher Andrew Macintyre
Art Director Karen Self
Publishing Director Jonathan Metcalf

DK INDIA
Senior Editors Vineetha Mokkil, Anita Kakar
Senior Art Editor Chhaya Sajwan
Project Editor Antara Moitra
Editors Agnibesh Das, Nisha Shaw, Seetha Natesh
Art Editors Namita, Heena Sharma, Sukriti Sobti, Shipra Jain
Assistant Editors Ira Pundeer, Ateendriya Gupta, Sneha Sunder Benjamin, Ankita Yadav
Assistant Art Editors Roshni Kapur, Meenal Goel, Priyansha Tuli, Aanchal Singhal
Illustrators Ivy Roy, Arun Pottirayil, Bharti Karakoti, Rahul Kumar
Managing Editor Pakshalika Jayaprakash
Managing Art Editor Arunesh Talapatra
Production Manager Pankaj Sharma
Pre-production Manager Balwant Singh
Senior DTP Designer Vishal Bhatia, Neeraj Bhatia
DTP Designer Sachin Gupta
Jacket Designer Surabhi Wadhwa
Managing Jackets Editor Saloni Singh
Senior DTP Designer (Jackets) Harish Aggarwal

This American Edition, 2024
First American Edition, 2016
Published in the United States by DK Publishing, a division of Penguin Random House LLC
1745 Broadway, 20th Floor, New York, NY 10019

Copyright © 2016, 2024 Dorling Kindersley Limited
24 25 26 27 28 10 9 8 7 6 5 4 3 2 1
001–339236–Jun/2024

A catalog record for this book is available from the Library of Congress.
ISBN 978-0-7440-9857-0

DK books are available at special discounts when purchased in bulk for sales promotions, premiums, fund-raising, or educational use. For details, contact: DK Publishing Special Markets, 1745 Broadway, 20th Floor, New York, NY 10019
SpecialSales@dk.com

Printed and bound in China

www.dk.com

This book was made with Forest Stewardship Council™ certified paper – one small step in DK's commitment to a sustainable future. Learn more at www.dk.com/uk/information/sustainability

Contents

How the course works

English for Everyone is designed for people who want to teach themselves the English language. Like all language courses, it covers the core skills: grammar, vocabulary, pronunciation, listening, speaking, reading, and writing. Unlike in other courses, the skills are taught and practiced as visually as possible, using images and graphics to help you understand and remember. The practice book is packed with exercises designed to reinforce the lessons you have learned in the course book. Work through the units in order, making full use of the audio available on the website and app.

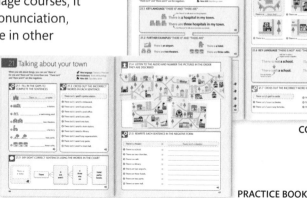

COURSE BOOK

PRACTICE BOOK

Unit number The book is divided into units. Each practice book unit tests the language taught in the course book unit with the same number.

Practice points Every unit begins with a summary of the key practice points.

Modules Each unit is broken down into modules, which should be done in order. You can take a break from learning after completing any module.

Vocabulary Throughout the book, vocabulary pages test your memory of key English words and phrases taught in the course book.

Visual practice Images and graphics offer visual cues to help fix the most useful and important English words in your memory.

09 Vocabulary

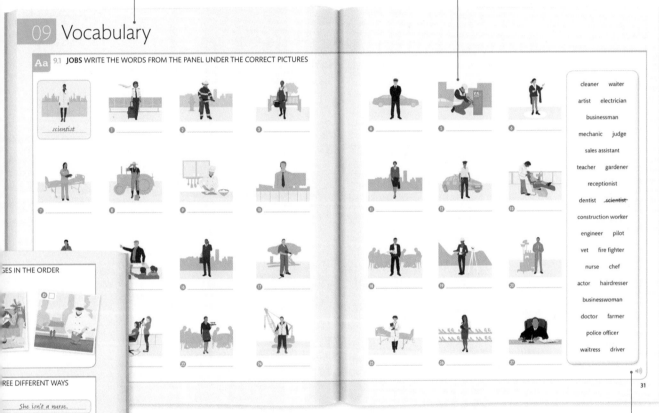

Aa 9.1 **JOBS** WRITE THE WORDS FROM THE PANEL UNDER THE CORRECT PICTURES

scientist

cleaner	waiter
artist	electrician
businessman	
mechanic	judge
sales assistant	
teacher	gardener
receptionist	
dentist	~~scientist~~
construction worker	
engineer	pilot
vet	fire fighter
nurse	chef
actor	hairdresser
businesswoman	
doctor	farmer
police officer	
waitress	driver

31

Audio support Most modules have supporting audio recordings of native English speakers to help you improve your speaking and listening skills.

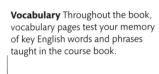

GES IN THE ORDER

REE DIFFERENT WAYS

She isn't a nurse.

My dad isn't at work.

Mia's blog
OME / ENTRIES / ABOUT / CONTACT
POSTED MONDAY, APRIL 20
My life
I'm Mia and I'm 47
ars old. I live in Los
geles, California, and
a chef. I work in a Mexican restaurant.
ot of people think I'm from Mexico, but
not. I'm from Colombia. I'm married
Franco. He's a carpenter. We have a son,
m. He studies at a local college.

FREE AUDIO
website and app
www.dkefe.com

9

Practice modules

Each exercise is carefully graded to drill and test the language taught in the corresponding course book units. Working through the exercises alongside the course book will help you remember what you have learned and become more fluent. Every exercise is introduced with a symbol to indicate which skill is being practiced.

GRAMMAR
Apply new language rules in different contexts.

READING
Examine target language in real-life English contexts.

LISTENING
Test your understanding of spoken English.

VOCABULARY
Cement your understanding of key vocabulary.

SPEAKING
Compare your spoken English to model audio recordings.

Module number Every module is identified with a unique number, so you can easily locate answers and related audio.

Exercise instruction Every exercise is introduced with a brief instruction, telling you what you need to do.

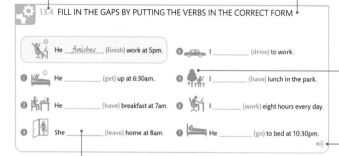

Supporting graphics Visual cues are given to help you understand the exercises.

Supporting audio This symbol shows that the answers to the exercise are available as audio tracks. Listen to them after completing the exercise.

Space for writing You are encouraged to write your answers in the book for future reference.

Speaking exercise This symbol indicates that you should say your answers out loud, then compare them to model recordings included in your audio files.

Listening exercise This symbol indicates that you should listen to an audio track in order to answer the questions in the exercise.

Sample answer The first question of each exercise is answered for you, to help make the task easy to understand.

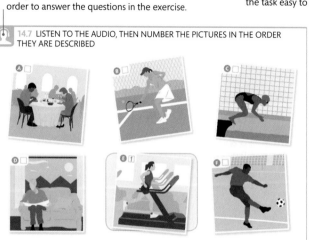

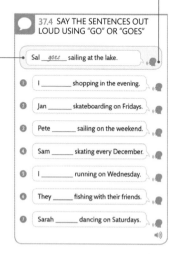

Audio

English for Everyone features extensive supporting audio materials. You are encouraged to use them as much as you can, to improve your understanding of spoken English, and to make your own accent and pronunciation more natural. Each file can be played, paused, and repeated as often as you like, until you are confident you understand what has been said.

LISTENING EXERCISES
This symbol indicates that you should listen to an audio track in order to answer the questions in the exercise.

SUPPORTING AUDIO
This symbol indicates that extra audio material is available for you to listen to after completing the module.

FREE AUDIO
website and app
www.dkefe.com

Answers

An answers section at the back of the book lists the correct answers for every exercise. Turn to these pages whenever you finish a module and compare your answers with the samples provided, to see how well you have understood each teaching point.

29

29.1 ◀))
❶ fork
❷ washing machine
❸ kettle
❹ toaster
❺ refrigerator
❻ sink
❼ plate

29.2 ◀))
❶ Does the house have a yard?
❷ Does their kitchen have a refrigerator?
❸ Does Bill's house have a big garage?
❹ Do you have a sofa?
❺ Does Barry have a kettle?
❻ Does she have a barbecue at her house?
❼ Does Marge have a new washing machine?
❽ Do Jack and Marienne have a TV?
❾ Does Leela's brother have a knife and fork?

29.3
❶ Claudia
❷ Paul
❸ Jenny
❹ Colin
❺ Roberto

29.4 ◀))
❶ Yes, I do.
❷ No, I don't.
❸ Yes, I do.
❹ Yes, I do.
❺ No, I don't.

29.5 ◀))
1. Do you have any chairs?
2. Do you have any knives?
3. Do you have a refrigerator?
4. Does he have any chairs?
5. Does he have any knives?
6. Does he have a refrigerator?
7. Do they have any chairs?
8. Do they have any knives?
9. Do they have a refrigerator?

29.6 ◀))
❶ Yes, **she does**.
❷ Yes, **he does**.

Answers Find the answers to every exercise printed at the back of the book.

Exercise numbers Match these numbers to the unique identifier at the top-left corner of each exercise.

Audio This symbol indicates that the answers can also be listened to.

01 Introducing yourself

You can greet people by saying "Hello!" or "Hi!" Introduce yourself using "I am." You may also need to spell out the letters of your name.

New language Using "to be" with names
Aa Vocabulary Names and letters
New skill Saying your name

1.1 REWRITE EACH SENTENCE IN ITS CONTRACTED FORM

> My name is Gary
> *My name's Gary.*

1. I am Natalie.

_____

2. My name is Sue.

_____

3. I am Ryan.

_____

4. My name is Mia.

_____

5. My name is Amelia.

_____

1.2 LISTEN TO THE AUDIO, THEN NUMBER THE PEOPLE IN THE ORDER YOU HEAR THEM SPEAK

A ☐ Rachel
B 1 Peter
C ☐ Jo
D ☐ Carl
E ☐ Terry
F ☐ Simone

1.3 USE THE CHART TO SAY 12 GREETINGS OUT LOUD

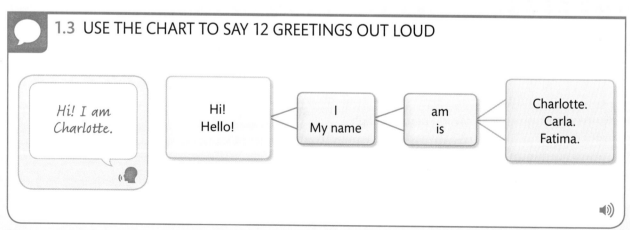

Hi! I am Charlotte.

| Hi! / Hello! | I / My name | am / is | Charlotte. Carla. Fatima. |

1.4 LISTEN TO THE AUDIO AND SPELL OUT THE NAMES YOU HEAR

R-A-C-H-E-L H-A-R-P-E-R

1. _____
2. _____
3. _____
4. _____
5. _____
6. _____
7. _____
8. _____
9. _____
10. _____
11. _____
12. _____
13. _____
14. _____
15. _____

1.5 SPELL OUT EACH PERSON'S NAME, THEN SAY THE SENTENCES OUT LOUD

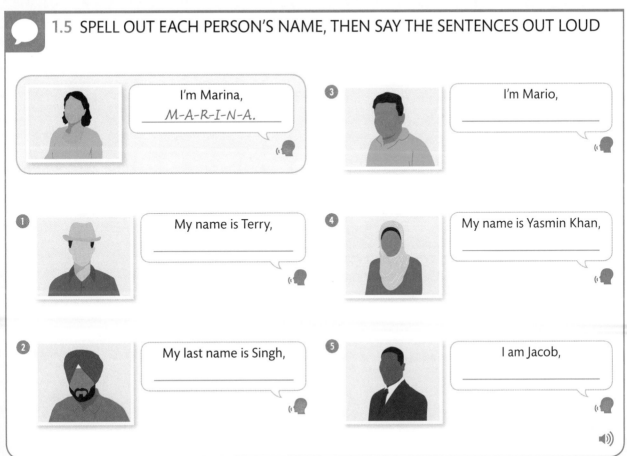

I'm Marina,
M-A-R-I-N-A.

3 I'm Mario,
_____

1 My name is Terry,
_____

4 My name is Yasmin Khan,
_____

2 My last name is Singh,
_____

5 I am Jacob,
_____

13

Aa 2.1 COUNTRIES WRITE THE COUNTRY NAMES FROM THE PANEL UNDER THE CORRECT FLAGS

Turkey

1 _____

2 _____

3 _____

4 _____

10 _____

11 _____

12 _____

13 _____

14 _____

20 _____

21 _____

22 _____

23 _____

24 _____

30 _____

31 _____

32 _____

33 _____

34 _____

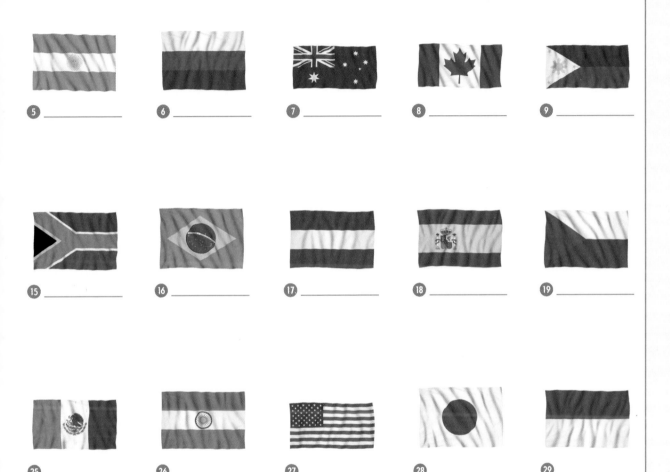

5 _____

6 _____

7 _____

8 _____

9 _____

15 _____

16 _____

17. _____

18 _____

19 _____

25 _____

26 _____

27 _____

28 _____

29 _____

Republic of Ireland   Greece   Singapore   France   Russia   Thailand   Argentina

South Africa   ~~Turkey~~   Mexico   New Zealand   Mongolia   China   Poland   India   Brazil

Egypt   Canada   Japan   Slovakia   Australia   Netherlands   Philippines   Portugal   Austria

South Korea   Spain   United Kingdom   Pakistan   Czech Republic

Indonesia   United Arab Emirates   Germany   United States of America   Switzerland

03 Talking about yourself

It's useful to know how to say your age and where you come from. You can use the verb "to be" to talk about these topics.

⚙ New language "To be" with ages and nationalities
Aa Vocabulary Numbers and nationalities
New skill Talking about yourself

Aa 3.1 WRITE EACH NUMBER AS A FIGURE

Three = _____3_____

1 Eighty-five = _____
2 Twenty-one = _____
3 Ninety = _____
4 Seventeen = _____
5 Eighty-four = _____

6 Sixty-two = _____
7 Forty-seven = _____
8 Fifty = _____
9 Seventy-one = _____
10 Twelve = _____
11 Thirty-three = _____

◀))

⚙ 3.2 REWRITE THE SENTENCES, CHANGING THE FIGURES TO WORDS

Pamela is 42 years old.
Pamela is forty-two years old.

1 Chloe is 31 years old.
_____

2 Heidi is 52 years old.
_____

3 Zach is 16 years old.
_____

4 Charlie is 10 years old.
_____

5 Marcel is 80 years old.
_____

6 Claire is 21 years old.
_____

7 Dan is 36 years old.
_____

8 Eleanor is 28 years old.
_____

9 Rebecca is 43 years old.
_____

◀))

3.3 USE THE CHART TO CREATE NINE CORRECT SENTENCES AND SAY THEM OUT LOUD

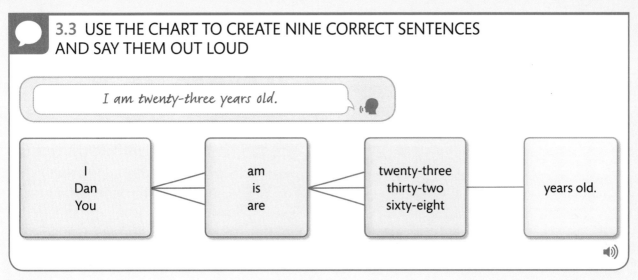

I am twenty-three years old.

I Dan You	am is are	twenty-three thirty-two sixty-eight	years old.

3.4 FILL IN THE GAPS WITH THE CORRECT FORMS OF "TO BE"

Alfonso _____*is*_____ 87 years old. He _____*is*_____ Spanish.

1 Abe _____ 72 years old. She _____ Japanese.

2 Mia and Leo _____ 12. They _____ from Italy.

3 Chantal _____ 66 years old. She _____ French.

4 Amir and Aamna _____ 90 years old. They _____ from Pakistan.

5 I _____ 24 years old. I _____ Irish.

6 Max _____ 47 years old. He _____ German.

7 We _____ 38 years old. We _____ from New Zealand.

8 My sister _____ 4 years old. She _____ from Canada.

Aa 4.1 PABLO'S FAMILY WRITE THE WORDS FROM THE PANEL IN THE CORRECT PLACES ON PABLO'S FAMILY TREE

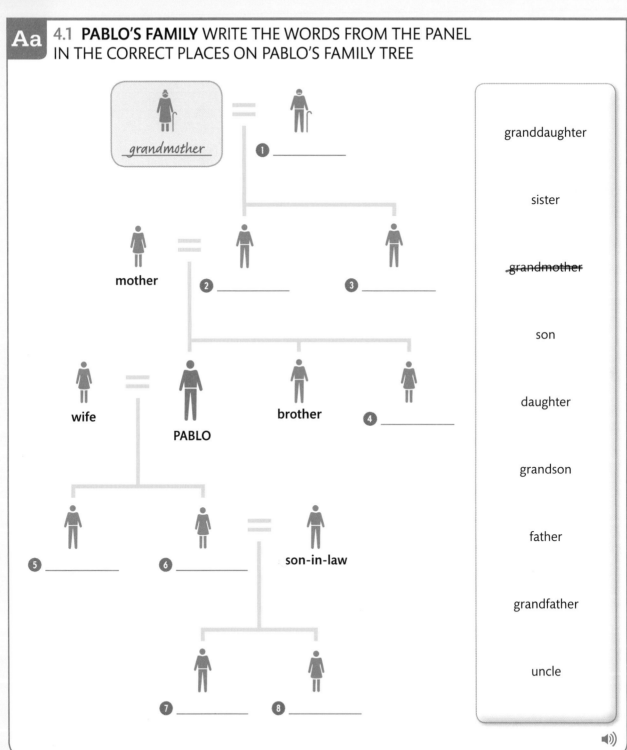

grandmother

① _____

mother

② _____

③ _____

wife

PABLO

brother

④ _____

⑤ _____

⑥ _____

son-in-law

⑦ _____

⑧ _____

granddaughter

sister

~~grandmother~~

son

daughter

grandson

father

grandfather

uncle

Aa 4.2 PETS AND DOMESTIC ANIMALS WRITE THE WORDS FROM THE PANEL UNDER THE CORRECT PICTURES

hamster

1 _____

2 _____

3 _____

4 _____

5 _____

6 _____

7 _____

8 _____

9 _____

10 _____

11 _____

guinea pig

parrot

dog

chicken

snake

~~hamster~~

cat

rabbit

fish

tortoise

pig

horse

05 Things you have

Possessive adjectives tell you who something (such as a pet) belongs to. "This" and "that" are determiners. They point out a specific object or person.

⚙ **New language** Possessive adjectives; "this" and "that"
Aa Vocabulary Animals and family
🧩 **New skill** Talking about who things belong to

5.1 FILL IN THE GAPS USING THE CORRECT POSSESSIVE ADJECTIVES

___Her___ (She) fish is called Nemo.

1 _____ (They) dog is called Beth.

2 _____ (He) tortoise is 50 years old.

3 _____ (I) cat is called Sam.

4 _____ (We) lion is from Kenya.

5 _____ (You) rabbit eats grass.

6 Here is _____ (it) bed.

7 _____ (They) snake is called Sid.

8 Buster is _____ (I) monkey.

9 _____ (You) parrot is from Venezuela.

10 _____ (She) cat is called Tabatha.

11 _____ (They) monkey is from Morocco.

12 _____ (She) pig lives on a farm.

13 _____ (He) horse is called Prancer.

14 _____ (We) chicken lives in the garden.

◀))

5.2 REWRITE THE SENTENCES, CORRECTING THE ERRORS

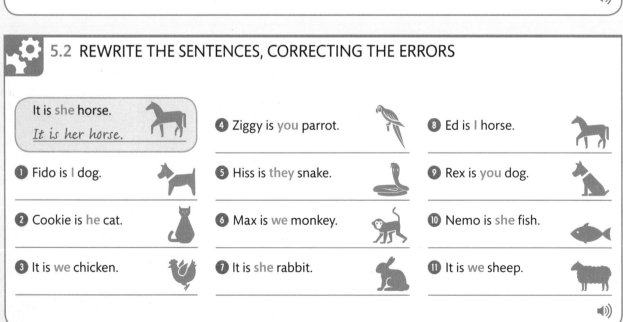

It is **she** horse.
It is her horse.

1 Fido is **I** dog.

2 Cookie is **he** cat.

3 It is **we** chicken.

4 Ziggy is **you** parrot.

5 Hiss is **they** snake.

6 Max is **we** monkey.

7 It is **she** rabbit.

8 Ed is **I** horse.

9 Rex is **you** dog.

10 Nemo is **she** fish.

11 It is **we** sheep.

◀))

5.3 FILL IN THE GAPS USING "THIS" OR "THAT"

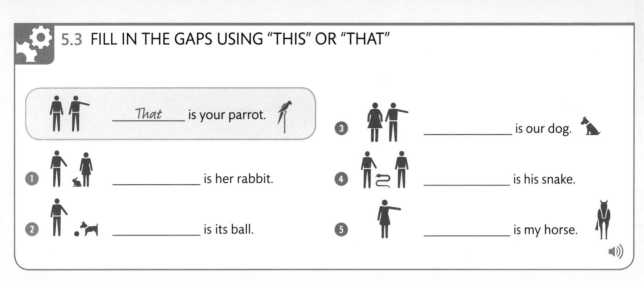

_____That_____ is your parrot.

1 _____ is her rabbit.

2 _____ is its ball.

3 _____ is our dog.

4 _____ is his snake.

5 _____ is my horse.

5.4 REWRITE THE SENTENCES, PUTTING THE WORDS IN THE CORRECT ORDER

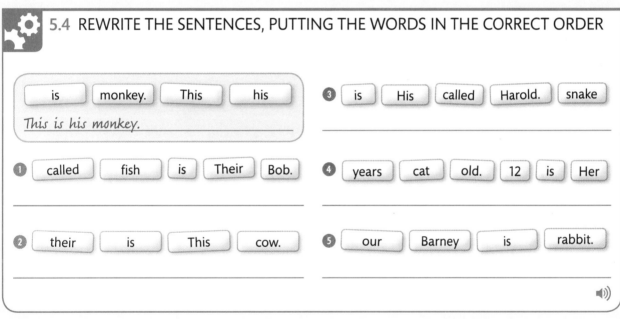

is | monkey. | This | his

This is his monkey.

1 called | fish | is | Their | Bob.

_____

2 their | is | This | cow.

_____

3 is | His | called | Harold. | snake

_____

4 years | cat | old. | 12 | is | Her

_____

5 our | Barney | is | rabbit.

_____

5.5 USE THE CHART TO CREATE 12 CORRECT SENTENCES AND SAY THEM OUT LOUD

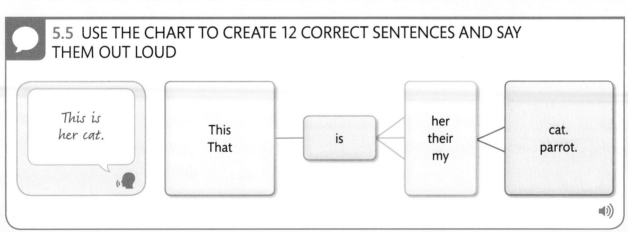

This is her cat.

| This / That | is | her / their / my | cat. / parrot. |

06 Using apostrophes

In English, you can use apostrophes (') to show belonging. You can use them to show who owns something, such as a pet, and to talk about your family.

⚙ **New language** Possessive apostrophe
Aa Vocabulary Family and pets
🧩 **New Skill** Talking about belonging

6.1 REWRITE THE PHRASES USING AN APOSTROPHE WITH "S"

	The son of Christopher	=	*Christopher's son*
①	The dog of Joe and Greg	=	
②	The granddaughters of Dolly	=	
③	The house of Sue	=	
④	The snake of Pete and Aziz	=	

6.2 LISTEN TO THE AUDIO AND MATCH THE PAIRS

	Angela is	Sam's mother.
①	Arthur is	Sam's grandfather.
②	Frank is	Sam's sister.
③	Charlotte is	Sam's grandmother.
④	Micky is	Sam's friend.
⑤	Sally is	Sam's father.
⑥	Ronaldo is	Sam's brother.
⑦	Rebecca is	Sam's cousin.

Angela is → Sam's grandmother.

6.3 READ THE ARTICLE AND ANSWER THE QUESTIONS

Sam lives with seven people.
True ☑ **False** ☐

❶ Esme is Sam's grandmother.
True ☐ **False** ☐

❷ Sam's mother is called Helen.
True ☐ **False** ☐

❸ Sam's sisters go to university.
True ☐ **False** ☐

❹ There are two animals in the family's home.
True ☐ **False** ☐

❺ Ted's snake is called Bouncer.
True ☐ **False** ☐

TELEVISION

A fascinating look at everyday life with the Douglas family

Sam Douglas lives with seven other people at his home in London. Esme and Alf are Sam's grandparents. They have 14 grandchildren. Sam's mom is called Annie; she works in the pub next to the family's house. Annie's husband is Ralf and he's a mechanic.

Sam has two sisters and one brother. His sisters are called Helen and Rebecca. They go to a school near their house. Ted is Sam's brother. He's 20 and goes to university.

There are two animals in the Douglas family's home. Bouncer is Sam's dog and Hiss is Ted's snake.

6.4 REWRITE THE SENTENCES, CORRECTING THE ERRORS

This is **Rogers'** house.
This is Roger's house.

❶ That's my **grandparent's** car.
_____

❷ These are **Pete and Omars'** cats.
_____

❸ I am **Sallys'** granddaughter.
_____

❹ Where is your **parent's** house?
_____

❺ Samantha is **Barrys'** new wife.
_____

🔊

6.5 SAY THE SENTENCES OUT LOUD, FILLING IN THE GAPS

Sally is ___*Fred's*___ (Fred) sister.
🗣

❶ Sooty is _____ (my brothers) cat.
🗣

❷ They are _____ (Tammy) parents.
🗣

❸ This is our _____ (children) snake.
🗣

❹ My _____ (parents) house is small.
🗣
🔊

Aa 7.1 **EVERYDAY THINGS** WRITE THE WORDS FROM THE PANEL UNDER THE CORRECT PICTURES

wallet

1 _____

2 _____

3 _____

7 _____

8 _____

9 _____

10 _____

14 _____

15 _____

16 _____

17 _____

21 _____

22 _____

23 _____

24 _____

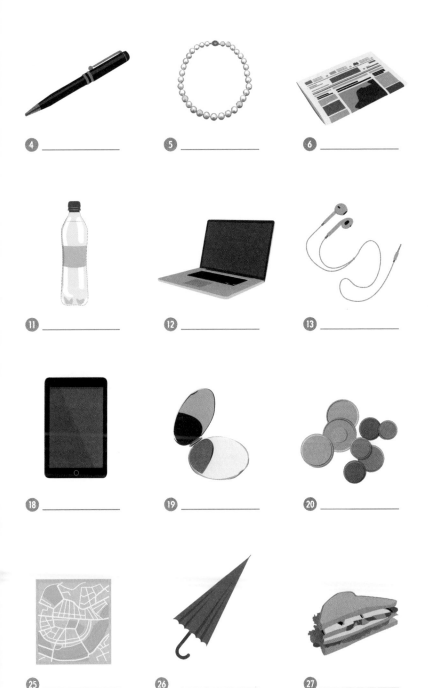

4 _____

5 _____

6 _____

11 _____

12 _____

13 _____

18 _____

19 _____

20 _____

25 _____

26 _____

27 _____

coins   dictionary

pencil   passport

camera   ID card

~~wallet~~   earphones

bottle of water   map

apple   notebook

tablet   toothbrush

sandwich   letter

mirror   sunglasses

keys   newspaper

hairbrush   necklace

book   glasses

laptop   umbrella

magazine   pen

08 Talking about your things

You use "these" and "those" when you are referring to more than one thing. To show who owns a thing, you can use determiners or possessive pronouns.

⚙ **New language** "These" and "those"
Aa Vocabulary Possessions
🧩 **New skill** Using determiners and pronouns

 8.1 CROSS OUT THE INCORRECT WORD IN EACH SENTENCE

This / ~~These~~ is my phone.

1 This / These are my mom's glasses.

2 That / Those are Samantha's keys.

3 This / These is Tom's umbrella.

4 This / These is my dog.

5 That / Those are Pete's books.

6 That / Those is your newspaper.

7 This / These are my tickets.

8 This / These are Marge's earrings.

9 This / These are his daughters.

10 That / Those is my teacher.

11 That / Those is your watch.

🔊

 8.2 REWRITE EACH SENTENCE IN ITS OTHER FORM

This is my sister.	These are my sisters.
1	These are my letters.
2 This is my purse.	
3	Those are Greg's keys.
4 That is my cat.	
5	These are my sister's pencils.
6 That is your dictionary.	
7 This is Dan's house.	
8	Those are Stan's books.
9	Those are my brothers.

8.3 REWRITE THE SINGULAR NOUNS IN THE PLURAL

apple = *apples*

1 pencil =
2 fish =
3 brother =
4 diary =
5 necklace =
6 brush =
7 watch =
8 box =
9 dictionary =
10 sister =
11 umbrella =
12 laptop =

🔊

8.4 REWRITE THE WORDS, CORRECTING THE SPELLINGS

diarys
diaries

1 brushs

2 boxs

3 dictionarys

4 doges

5 notebookses

6 toothbrushs

7 bookes

8 penciles

9 lettres

10 newspaperes

11 glasss

12 passportes

13 magazinees

🔊

Aa 8.5 WRITE DOWN WHAT EACH PICTURE SHOWS

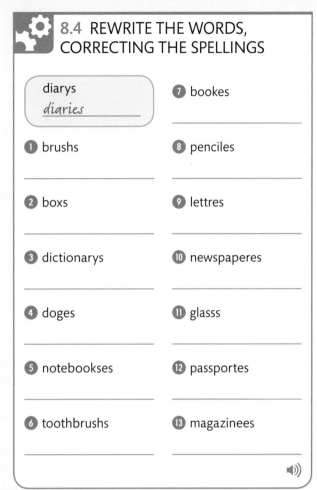

four books

1 _____

2 _____

3 _____

4 _____

5 _____

6 _____

7 _____

Aa 8.6 MATCH THE DETERMINERS TO THE PRONOUNS

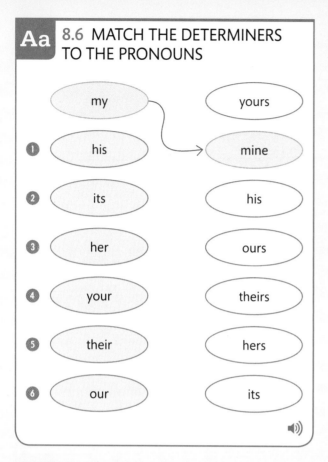

my — mine

1 his — mine

2 its

3 her

4 your

yours

his

ours

theirs

hers

its

8.7 REWRITE CHANGING THE DETERMINERS TO PRONOUNS

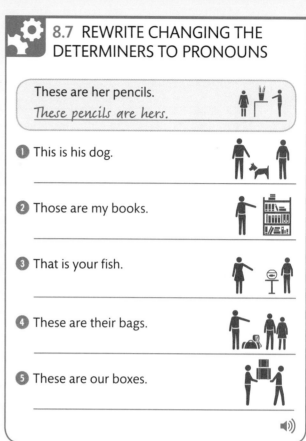

These are her pencils.
These pencils are hers.

1 This is his dog.
_____

2 Those are my books.
_____

3 That is your fish.
_____

4 These are their bags.
_____

5 These are our boxes.
_____

8.8 LISTEN TO THE AUDIO AND MARK THE SENTENCES YOU HEAR

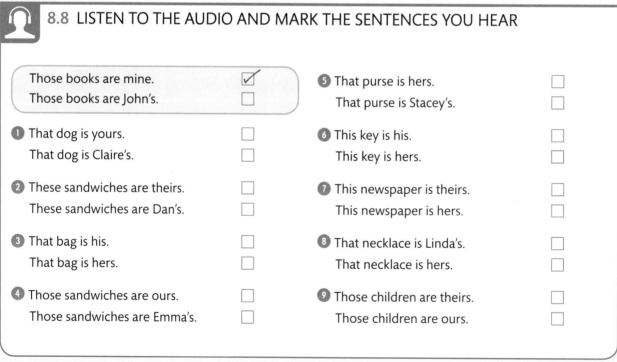

Those books are mine. ☑
Those books are John's. ☐

1 That dog is yours. ☐
That dog is Claire's. ☐

2 These sandwiches are theirs. ☐
These sandwiches are Dan's. ☐

3 That bag is his. ☐
That bag is hers. ☐

4 Those sandwiches are ours. ☐
Those sandwiches are Emma's. ☐

5 That purse is hers. ☐
That purse is Stacey's. ☐

6 This key is his. ☐
This key is hers. ☐

7 This newspaper is theirs. ☐
This newspaper is hers. ☐

8 That necklace is Linda's. ☐
That necklace is hers. ☐

9 Those children are theirs. ☐
Those children are ours. ☐

8.9 SAY THE SENTENCES OUT LOUD, FILLING IN THE GAPS USING "THIS" AND "THESE"

These are my pencils.

1. _____ are my books.

2. _____ is your dog.

3. _____ are her bags.

4. _____ are their boxes.

5. _____ is my toothbrush.

6. _____ is his diary.

7. _____ is your apple.

8. _____ are my apples.

9. _____ are your glasses.

10. _____ are Kevin's keys.

11. _____ is my dad's car.

Aa 8.10 WRITE THE DETERMINERS AND PRONOUNS FROM THE EMAIL IN THE CORRECT GROUPS

DETERMINERS

_____
_____
_____

PRONOUNS

_____
_____

To: Samantha

Subject: A new pet

Hi Samantha,

How are you? Thank you for your email. I have some big news: I have a new dog. His name is Rex and he is very big. I take him for a walk in the evening with my girlfriend Jane. Jane has a dog, too, but hers is very small. His name is Fido. Jane's dog likes mine!

We go to the park with our dogs every day. It's fun.

Let's meet soon,
Tim

09 Vocabulary

Aa 9.1 JOBS WRITE THE WORDS FROM THE PANEL UNDER THE CORRECT PICTURES

scientist

1 _____

2 _____

3 _____

7 _____

8 _____

9 _____

10 _____

14 _____

15 _____

16 _____

17 _____

21 _____

22 _____

23 _____

24 _____

4 _____

5 _____

6 _____

11 _____

12 _____

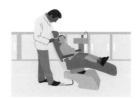

13 _____

18 _____

19 _____

20 _____

25 _____

26 _____

27 _____

cleaner   waiter

artist   electrician

businessman

mechanic   judge

sales assistant

teacher   gardener

receptionist

dentist   ~~scientist~~

construction worker

engineer   pilot

vet   fire fighter

nurse   chef

actor   hairdresser

businesswoman

doctor   farmer

police officer

waitress   driver

10 Talking about your job

You can use the verb "to be" to describe your job. The verb "to work" gives more information about where you work and who you work with.

New language Using "I am" for your job
Aa Vocabulary Jobs and workplaces
New skill Describing your job

10.1 REWRITE EACH SENTENCE IN ITS OTHER FORM

I am an actor.   *We are actors.*

1. _____   They are doctors.

2. You are a teacher.   _____

3. _____   We are hairdressers.

4. I am a mechanic.   _____

5. _____   You are cleaners.

6. She is a chef.   _____

7. _____   They are actors.

8. He is a vet.   _____

9. _____   We are police officers.

10. You are a farmer.   _____

11. _____   You are waitresses.

12. I am a gardener.   _____

13. _____   We are artists.

10.2 FILL IN THE GAPS WITH THE CORRECT VERBS AND ARTICLES

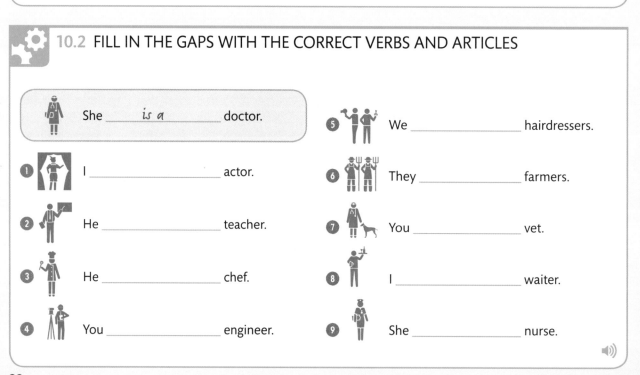

She _____*is a*_____ doctor.

1. I _____ actor.

2. He _____ teacher.

3. He _____ chef.

4. You _____ engineer.

5. We _____ hairdressers.

6. They _____ farmers.

7. You _____ vet.

8. I _____ waiter.

9. She _____ nurse.

10.3 CROSS OUT THE INCORRECT WORD IN EACH SENTENCE

They ~~is~~ / are gardeners.

1 I am / is a vet.

2 She is / are a businesswoman.

3 We is / are doctors.

4 They is / are teachers.

5 He is / are a mechanic.

6 I am / is a driver.

7 We am / are receptionists.

8 They are / is waitresses.

9 She is / are a police officer.

10 I am / is a judge.

11 You is / are a nurse.

12 We am / are farmers.

13 She is / are a sales assistant.

14 I am / are a chef.

Aa 10.4 MATCH THE PICTURES TO THE CORRECT LABELS

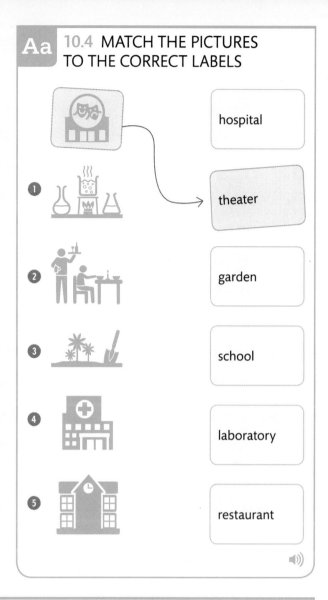

hospital

theater

garden

school

laboratory

restaurant

 ## 10.5 CROSS OUT THE INCORRECT WORD IN EACH SENTENCE

I work ~~on~~ / in an office.

1 He works on / in a doctor's office.

2 We work on / in a farm.

3 My dad works on / in a building site.

4 My sister works on / in a café.

5 We work on / in people's gardens.

6 Dan works on / in a hospital.

7 I work on / in a restaurant.

8 We work on / in a school.

9 Chris works on / in a supermarket.

10.6 LOOK AT THE PICTURES AND SAY THE SENTENCES OUT LOUD, USING THE WORDS IN THE PANEL

Eric _____*is a waiter.*_____
He _*works in a restaurant.*_

1

Abby _____
She _____

2

Julie _____
She _____

3

Simon _____
He _____

4

Adam _____
He _____

5

Max _____
He _____

6

Carol _____
She _____

~~waiter~~   police officer   park   nurse

hairdresser   ~~restaurant~~   engineer

police station   hospital

beauty salon   gardener   farm

construction site   farmer

10.7 FILL IN THE GAPS USING THE WORDS IN THE PANEL

Peter is a _____teacher_____ ( ) and he works with _____children_____ ( ).

1 Sam is a _____ ( ) and she works with _____ ( ).

2 Gabriella is a _____ ( ) and she works with _____ ( ).

3 Dan is a _____ ( ) and he works with _____ ( ).

4 John is a _____ ( ) and he works with _____ ( ).

5 Tom is an _____ ( ) and he works in a _____ ( ).

doctor	crops	theater	patients	chef	~~children~~
~~teacher~~	animals	food	vet	farmer	actor

10.8 LISTEN TO THE AUDIO AND ANSWER THE QUESTIONS

Pete is a...
farmer. ☑ contractor. ☐ gardener. ☐

1 Simon is a...
contractor. ☐ gardener. ☐ teacher. ☐

2 Sue is a...
nurse. ☐ chef. ☐ teacher. ☐

3 John is a...
scientist. ☐ businessman. ☐ doctor. ☐

4 Alberto is a...
waiter. ☐ chef. ☐ actor. ☐

5 Susan and Pam are...
chefs. ☐ hairdressers. ☐ gardeners. ☐

6 Douglas is an...
actor. ☐ farmer. ☐ police officer. ☐

7 Danny is a...
contractor. ☐ architect. ☐ farmer. ☐

11 Telling the time

There are two ways of saying the time. You can use hours and minutes, or you can say the minutes first and state their relation to the hour.

⚙ **New language** Times of the day
Aa Vocabulary Words for time
🧩 **New skill** Saying what the time is

Aa 11.1 MATCH THE PICTURES TO THE CORRECT TIMES

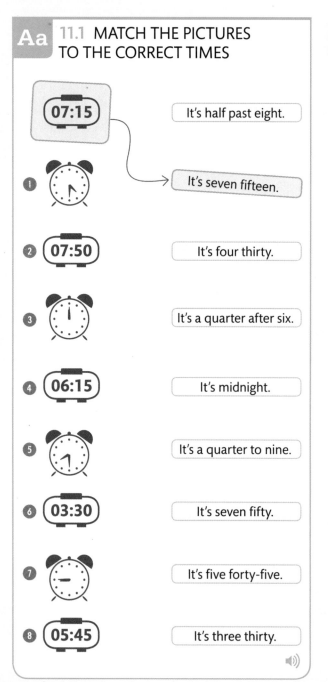

07:15 → It's seven fifteen.

It's half past eight.

1 — It's seven fifteen.

2 07:50 — It's four thirty.

3 — It's a quarter after six.

4 06:15 — It's midnight.

5 — It's a quarter to nine.

6 03:30 — It's seven fifty.

7 — It's five forty-five.

8 05:45 — It's three thirty.

🔊

🎧 **11.2 LISTEN TO THE AUDIO AND MARK THE CORRECT TIMES**

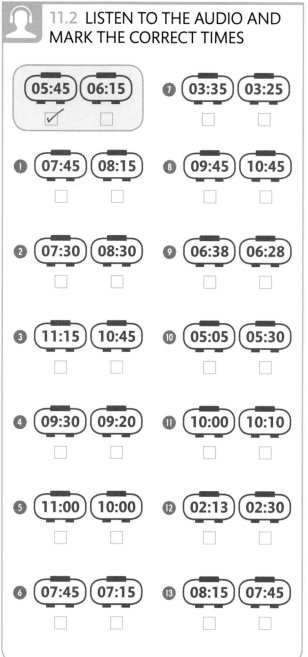

05:45 ✓ 06:15 ☐

1 07:45 ☐ 08:15 ☐   8 09:45 ☐ 10:45 ☐

2 07:30 ☐ 08:30 ☐   9 06:38 ☐ 06:28 ☐

3 11:15 ☐ 10:45 ☐   10 05:05 ☐ 05:30 ☐

4 09:30 ☐ 09:20 ☐   11 10:00 ☐ 10:10 ☐

5 11:00 ☐ 10:00 ☐   12 02:13 ☐ 02:30 ☐

6 07:45 ☐ 07:15 ☐   13 08:15 ☐ 07:45 ☐

7 03:35 ☐ 03:25 ☐

11.3 REWRITE THE TIMES USING FIGURES

It's a quarter to six. = 05:45

1 It's a quarter past eleven. = _____

2 It's eleven o'clock. = _____

3 It's eight twenty-four. = _____

4 It's half past three. = _____

5 It's a quarter to three. = _____

6 It's five twenty-five. = _____

7 It's three forty-nine. = _____

8 It's two fifteen. = _____

9 It's nine o'clock. = _____

10 It's a quarter to eight. = _____

11 It's half past eleven. = _____

12 It's nine twenty-five. = _____

13 It's a quarter after ten. = _____

14 It's eleven twenty. = _____

15 It's one fifty-five. = _____

16 It's quarter to seven. = _____

17 It's six forty-five. = _____

11.4 LOOK AT THE PICTURES, THEN SAY EACH TIME OUT LOUD

09:15 It's a quarter past nine.

1 **09:45** _____

2 **04:00** _____

3 **10:20** _____

4 **11:30** _____

5 **03:47** _____

6 **03:15** _____

7 **06:30** _____

8 **08:22** _____

9 **01:25** _____

12 Vocabulary

go to work

1 _____

2 _____

3 _____

7 _____

8 _____

9 _____

10 _____

14 _____

15 _____

16 _____

17 _____

21 _____

22 _____

23 _____

24 _____

38

4 _____

5 _____

6 _____

11 _____

12 _____

13 _____

18 _____

19 _____

20 _____

25 _____

26 _____

27 _____

start work   clear the table

wash your face   wake up

go to bed   cook dinner

~~go to work~~   iron a shirt

leave work   get dressed

do the dishes   have dinner

go to school   walk the dog

buy groceries   take a shower

dawn   have lunch   get up

brush your teeth   go home

day   finish work   dusk

brush your hair   take a bath

have breakfast   night

13 Describing your day

Use the present simple tense to talk about the things you do regularly: for example, when you normally go to work or eat lunch.

New language The present simple
Aa Vocabulary Routine activities
New skill Talking about your daily routine

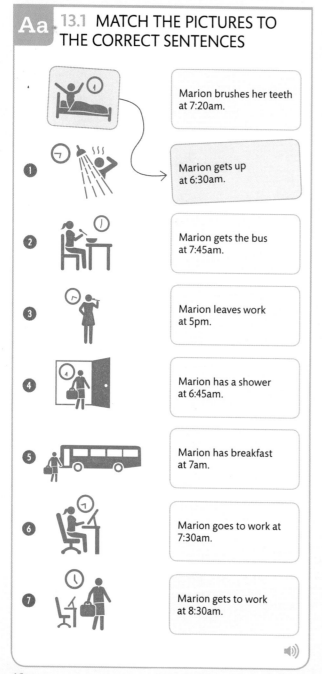

Aa 13.1 MATCH THE PICTURES TO THE CORRECT SENTENCES

Marion brushes her teeth at 7:20am.

Marion gets up at 6:30am.

Marion gets the bus at 7:45am.

Marion leaves work at 5pm.

Marion has a shower at 6:45am.

Marion has breakfast at 7am.

Marion goes to work at 7:30am.

Marion gets to work at 8:30am.

13.2 CROSS OUT THE INCORRECT WORD IN EACH SENTENCE

She eats / ~~eat~~ dinner in the evening.

1. I wake / wakes up at 6:30am.
2. He gets / get up at 6am.
3. She have / has a shower at 7am.
4. They have / has cereal for breakfast.
5. He have / has a shower before breakfast.
6. She leaves / leave home at 7:15am.
7. The bus go / goes every half hour.
8. I get / gets to work at 8:30am.
9. He start / starts work at 9am.
10. She take / takes an hour for lunch.
11. I go / goes to the sandwich shop for lunch.
12. They eat / eats lunch in the canteen.
13. He finish / finishes work at 5pm.
14. They go / goes home on the bus.
15. He wash / washes his car every weekend.
16. I watch / watches TV after dinner.
17. They go / goes to bed at 11pm.
18. He sleep / sleeps for eight hours.

13.3 FILL IN THE GAPS BY PUTTING THE VERBS IN THE CORRECT FORM

| I eat | = | She _____*eats*_____ |

1 I have = He _____

2 I start = It _____

3 I leave = He _____

4 I get up = She _____

5 I go = It _____

6 I wake up = She _____

7 I wash = He _____

8 I watch = She _____

9 I finish = It _____

 13.4 FILL IN THE GAPS BY PUTTING THE VERBS IN THE CORRECT FORM

He _____ *finishes* (finish) work at 5pm.

1 He _____ (get) up at 6:30am.

2 He _____ (have) breakfast at 7am.

3 She _____ (leave) home at 8am.

4 I _____ (drive) to work.

5 I _____ (have) lunch in the park.

6 I _____ (work) eight hours every day.

7 He _____ (go) to bed at 10:30pm.

13.5 SAY THESE VERBS OUT LOUD

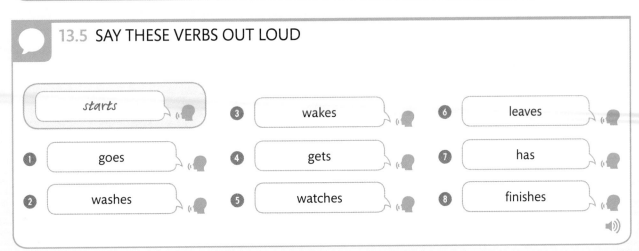

starts

1 goes

2 washes

3 wakes

4 gets

5 watches

6 leaves

7 has

8 finishes

41

14 Describing your week

You can talk about your usual weekly activities using the present simple with time phrases. Time phrases are often formed using prepositions and days of the week.

⚙ **New language** Days and prepositions
Aa Vocabulary Days of the week
🧩 **New skill** Talking about your weekly routine

14.1 FILL IN THE GAPS USING THE WORDS "ON" AND "IN"

Peter plays soccer __on__ Sundays.

1 I go to the movies _____ the weekend.

2 Joe starts work at 6pm _____ Mondays.

3 You watch TV _____ the afternoon.

4 Harry plays tennis _____ Wednesdays.

5 Lin goes swimming _____ the evening.

6 Alex goes fishing _____ the weekend.

7 He eats lunch at 1pm _____ Fridays.

8 Sam goes to the gym _____ the morning.

🔊

14.2 MARK THE SENTENCES THAT ARE CORRECT

I play soccer on Mondays. ☑
I play soccer at Mondays. ☐

1 I work from Monday to Thursday. ☐
I work of Monday to Thursday. ☐

2 My sister go swimming every day. ☐
My sister goes swimming every day. ☐

3 We go to the gym on Saturdays. ☐
We go to the gym at Saturdays. ☐

4 You read the newspaper in Sundays. ☐
You read the newspaper on Sundays. ☐

5 Peter goes to work on the weekend. ☐
Peter goes to work from the weekend. ☐

6 Jennifer goes to a café for Fridays. ☐
Jennifer goes to a café on Fridays. ☐

7 Sam and Pete work to 9am from 5pm. ☐
Sam and Pete work from 9am to 5pm. ☐

🔊

14.3 SAY THE SENTENCES OUT LOUD, FILLING IN THE GAPS

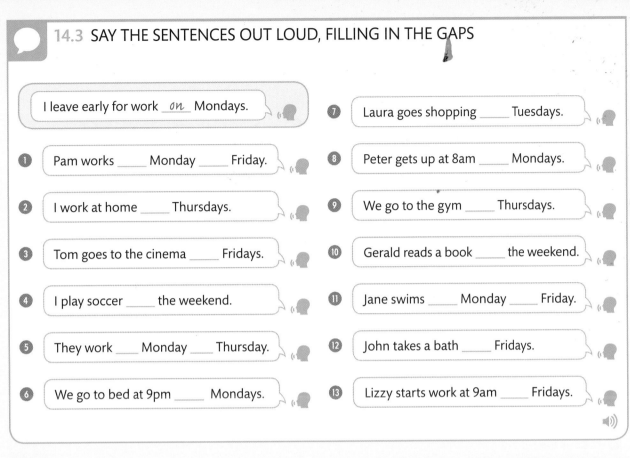

I leave early for work _on_ Mondays.

1 Pam works _____ Monday _____ Friday.

2 I work at home _____ Thursdays.

3 Tom goes to the cinema _____ Fridays.

4 I play soccer _____ the weekend.

5 They work _____ Monday _____ Thursday.

6 We go to bed at 9pm _____ Mondays.

7 Laura goes shopping _____ Tuesdays.

8 Peter gets up at 8am _____ Mondays.

9 We go to the gym _____ Thursdays.

10 Gerald reads a book _____ the weekend.

11 Jane swims _____ Monday _____ Friday.

12 John takes a bath _____ Fridays.

13 Lizzy starts work at 9am _____ Fridays.

14.4 REWRITE THE SENTENCES, PUTTING THE WORDS IN THE CORRECT ORDER

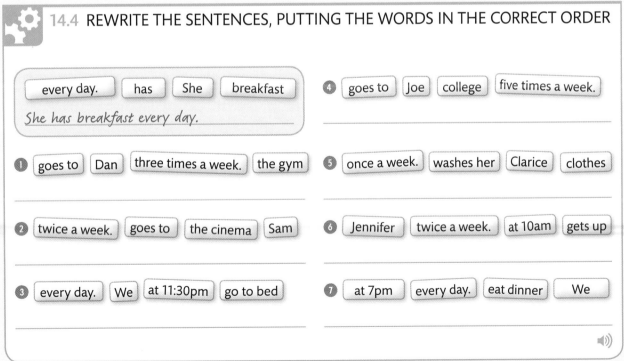

every day. has She breakfast

She has breakfast every day.

1 goes to Dan three times a week. the gym

_____

2 twice a week. goes to the cinema Sam

_____

3 every day. We at 11:30pm go to bed

_____

4 goes to Joe college five times a week.

_____

5 once a week. washes her Clarice clothes

_____

6 Jennifer twice a week. at 10am gets up

_____

7 at 7pm every day. eat dinner We

_____

14.5 REWRITE THE SENTENCES, CORRECTING THE ERRORS

I **wakes up** at 6:30am.
I wake up at 6:30am.

1 Bob **go swimming** on Thursdays.

2 I play tennis **on weekend**.

3 Jane and Tom go to the gym **three time** a week.

4 Angus works from **Monday on Thursday**.

5 I go to the movies **on weekend**.

6 Sam goes to **college Wednesdays**.

7 Jenny gets up **in 7am** every day.

8 Peter **work from** Monday to Friday.

9 Nina **go to bed** at 11pm every day.

14.6 READ THE EMAIL AND ANSWER THE QUESTIONS

Jim goes to the gym three times a week.
True ☐ **False** ☑

1 Jim goes to work at 6am.
True ☐ **False** ☐

2 Jim goes to the gym on Mondays and Tuesdays.
True ☐ **False** ☐

3 He plays soccer on Fridays.
True ☐ **False** ☐

4 Jim and his wife get up at 10am on the weekend.
True ☐ **False** ☐

5 They go to the theater on Saturdays.
True ☐ **False** ☐

6 They go to a restaurant on Sundays.
True ☐ **False** ☐

To: Pete

Subject: My week

Hi Pete,
Let me tell you about my typical week. From Monday to Thursday, I get up early, at 6am. I eat breakfast, then I go to work at 8:30am. On Fridays, I work at home. I like Fridays. I like sports a lot. I go to the gym twice a week, on Mondays and Tuesdays, and I go swimming on Wednesdays. I play soccer on Thursdays, but I relax on Friday and read a newspaper.

On the weekend, my wife and I get up at 10am. We go to the movies on Saturdays, and on Sundays, we go to a good restaurant. Tell me about your weekend!

Jim

14.7 LISTEN TO THE AUDIO, THEN NUMBER THE PICTURES IN THE ORDER THEY ARE DESCRIBED

A ☐

B ☐

C ☐

D ☐

E ☐ 1

F ☐

 14.8 LISTEN TO 14.7 AGAIN AND ANSWER THE QUESTIONS

Kate goes to the gym on...
Monday ☐ **Tuesday** ☐ **Friday** ✓

❶ Paul is a...
farmer ☐ **teacher** ☐ **doctor** ☐

❷ Jane is a...
nurse ☐ **doctor** ☐ **teacher** ☐

❸ On the weekend, Jane goes to...
a restaurant ☐ **the movies** ☐ **a gym** ☐

❹ Sally gets up at...
6am ☐ **7am** ☐ **8am** ☐

❺ Sally goes swimming on...
Saturday ☐ **Sunday** ☐ **Thursday** ☐

❻ Eric works at the...
school ☐ **theater** ☐ **restaurant** ☐

❼ Eric works... a week.
twice ☐ **three days** ☐ **four days** ☐

❽ Claire is a...
waitress ☐ **carpenter** ☐ **farmer** ☐

❾ Claire starts work at...
6am ☐ **4pm** ☐ **6pm** ☐

15 Negatives with "to be"

You make a sentence negative by using "not" or its short form "-n't." Negative sentences with the verb "to be" have different rules than negatives with other verbs.

⚙ **New language** Negatives with "to be"
Aa Vocabulary "Not"
🧩 **New skill** Saying what things are not

15.1 REWRITE THE SENTENCES, PUTTING THE WORDS IN THE CORRECT ORDER

o'clock. | 5 | not | is | It
It is not 5 o'clock.

① teacher. | Paula | not | is | a
_____

② are | not | England. | We | from
_____

③ my | This | phone. | not | is
_____

④ years | Kirsty | not | old. | 18 | is
_____

⑤ is | not | Frank | my | father.
_____

⑥ This | my | not | purse. | is
_____

⑦ not | They | are | engineers.
_____

⑧ is | That | salon. | not | a
_____

⑨ Kim | a | teacher. | is | not
_____

🔊

15.2 FILL IN THE GAPS TO MAKE NEGATIVE SENTENCES

They _____ *are not* _____ hairdressers.

① That _____ a castle.

② They _____ at school.

③ He _____ a grandfather.

④ We _____ engineers.

⑤ She _____ 70 years old.

⑥ You _____ French.

⑦ This _____ my dog.

⑧ I _____ a doctor.

⑨ It _____ 11 o'clock.

🔊

15.3 LISTEN TO THE AUDIO, THEN NUMBER THE IMAGES IN THE ORDER THEY ARE DESCRIBED

A ☐

B 1

C ☐

D ☐

15.4 FILL IN THE GAPS TO WRITE EACH SENTENCE THREE DIFFERENT WAYS

She is not a nurse.	She's not a nurse.	She isn't a nurse.
1 _____	Fredo's not a chef.	_____
2 Susie is not my cat.	_____	_____
3 _____	_____	My dad isn't at work.
4 _____	They're not at the theater.	_____

15.5 READ THE BLOG AND ANSWER THE QUESTIONS

Mia is 45 years old.	True ☐	False ☑
1 She lives in California.	True ☐	False ☐
2 She's a waitress in a restaurant.	True ☐	False ☐
3 She isn't Mexican.	True ☐	False ☐
4 Franco isn't an engineer.	True ☐	False ☐
5 They have a daughter in college.	True ☐	False ☐

Mia's blog

HOME | ENTRIES | ABOUT | CONTACT

POSTED MONDAY, APRIL 20
My life

Hi! I'm Mia and I'm 47 years old. I live in Los Angeles, California, and I'm a chef. I work in a Mexican restaurant. A lot of people think I'm from Mexico, but I'm not. I'm from Colombia. I'm married to Franco. He's a carpenter. We have a son, Sam. He studies at a local college.

15.6 REWRITE THE SENTENCES, CORRECTING THE ERRORS

This **aren't** your cat.
This isn't your cat.

1 This **aren't** his umbrella.

_____

2 Pedro **aren't** Spanish.

_____

3 Pete and Terry **isn't** hairdressers.

_____

4 It **aren't** a snake.

_____

5 My cousins **isn't** 21 years old.

_____

6 It **aren't** half past six.

_____

7 I **isn't** your friend.

_____

🔊

15.7 READ THE BLOG AND ANSWER THE QUESTIONS

Theresa is not from Germany.
True ☐ **False** ☑

1 Lucia is not 41 years old.
True ☐ **False** ☐

2 There isn't a learner from Spain.
True ☐ **False** ☐

3 Pablo is not a teacher.
True ☐ **False** ☐

4 Theresa is not a teacher.
True ☐ **False** ☐

5 Xi is not a chef.
True ☐ **False** ☐

6 Xi does not live in China.
True ☐ **False** ☐

< > ||| 🔍 ⌂ C

For learners

HOME | ENTRIES | ABOUT | FORUM

POSTED FRIDAY, JUNE 18
INTRODUCE YOURSELF

THERESA GEISSLER
Hi, my name's Theresa. I'm a student from Germany, and I'm 17 years old.

LUCIA ALONSO
Hello, everyone. I am from Italy, and my name is Lucia. I am 42, and I am an engineer.

PABLO MONTOYA
I am a teacher called Pablo. I come from Argentina. I am 51, and I have been learning English for the last six months.

XI LIU
Hello, my name is Xi. I am 32 years old. I am a doctor, and I live with my wife and son in China.

15.8 TURN THE "YOU" STATEMENTS INTO "I" STATEMENTS

> You're a nurse. You're not a doctor.
> *I'm a nurse. I'm not a doctor.*

❶ You're a student. You're not a teacher.

❷ You're 30 years old. You're not 40.

❸ You're a farmer. You're not a police officer.

❹ You're French. You're not English.

❺ You're an uncle. You're not a father.

❻ You're 18. You're not 21.

❼ You're a waitress. You're not a chef.

❽ You're Spanish. You're not Italian.

15.9 TURN THE "I" STATEMENTS INTO "YOU" STATEMENTS

> I'm French. I'm not German.
> *You're French. You're not German.*

❶ I'm 28. I'm not 29.

❷ I'm a scientist. I'm not a gardener.

❸ I'm Austrian. I'm not English.

❹ I'm a contractor. I'm not an actor.

❺ I'm 16. I'm not 18.

❻ I'm an uncle. I'm not a grandfather.

❼ I'm a mechanic. I'm not an engineer.

❽ I'm a police officer. I'm not a firefighter.

15.10 USE THE CHART TO CREATE 12 CORRECT SENTENCES AND SAY THEM OUT LOUD

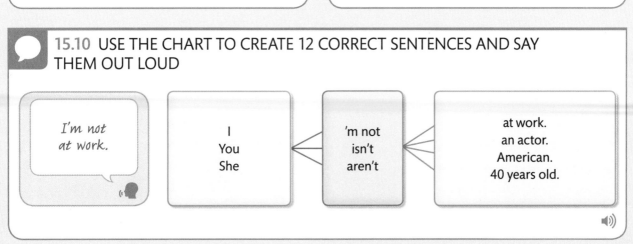

I'm not at work.

I	'm not	at work.
You	isn't	an actor.
She	aren't	American.
		40 years old.

16 More negatives

For most verbs in English, add "do not" or "does not" before the verb to make it negative. This is often shortened to "don't" or "doesn't."

⚙ **New language** Present simple negative
Aa Vocabulary Daily activities
New skill Saying what you don't do

16.1 FILL IN THE GAPS USING "DO NOT" OR "DOES NOT"

She __*does not*__ play tennis on Wednesdays.

1 Jane _____ walk to work.

2 My brother _____ watch TV.

3 I _____ read a book in the evening.

4 Frank _____ work at the museum.

5 They _____ go dancing on the weekend.

6 We _____ go to work on Fridays.

7 I _____ get up at 7:30am.

8 You _____ have a car.

9 My dad _____ work in an office.

10 You _____ have a dog.

11 My sister _____ work with children.

12 They _____ live in the country.

13 Freddie _____ eat meat.

🔊

16.2 REWRITE THE SENTENCES, PUTTING THE WORDS IN THE CORRECT ORDER

go | Mick | on Wednesdays. | to work | doesn't
Mick doesn't go to work on Wednesdays.

1 in New York. | live | doesn't | Tony
_____

2 doesn't | a farm. | work | on | Sebastian
_____

3 a factory. | doesn't | uncle | My | in | work
_____

4 on Thursdays. | soccer | play | We | don't
_____

5 German | don't | at school. | I | learn
_____

6 work | Carlo | on Mondays. | doesn't
_____

7 don't | at | You | take | a bath | night.
_____

🔊

16.3 WRITE TWO NEGATIVE FORMS OF EACH SENTENCE

I get up at 7am.	*I do not get up at 7am.*	*I don't get up at 7am.*
1 Tim plays tennis.		
2 You have a black cat.		
3 Jules reads a book every day.		
4 Sam works in a restaurant.		
5 They play soccer.		
6 Emily works with animals.		
7 Mel and Greg have a car.		
8 You work in a factory.		

16.4 REWRITE THE SENTENCES, CORRECTING THE ERRORS

He don't go swimming on Wednesdays.
He doesn't go swimming on Wednesdays.

1 Chloe don't play tennis with her friends.

_____

2 You doesn't work outside.

_____

3 Sal and Doug doesn't have a car.

_____

4 We doesn't watch TV at home.

_____

5 Mrs. O'Brien don't work in an office.

_____

6 You doesn't wake up at 6am.

_____

7 They doesn't eat lunch at 1pm.

_____

8 Virginia don't speak good English.

_____

9 Trevor don't live near here.

_____

10 My dad don't live in Los Angeles.

_____

11 David don't play chess.

_____

Aa 16.5 MARK THE SENTENCES THAT ARE CORRECT

Jenny doesn't work in a bank. ☑
Jenny don't work in a bank. ☐

1 Jean don't cycle to work. ☐
Jean doesn't cycle to work. ☐

2 They don't live in the city. ☐
They doesn't live in the city. ☐

3 Mr. James don't go to the theater. ☐
Mr. James doesn't go to the theater. ☐

4 He doesn't read a newspaper. ☐
He don't read a newspaper. ☐

5 My cousins don't have tickets. ☐
My cousins doesn't have tickets. ☐

6 Sally doesn't go to the gym. ☐
Sally don't go to the gym. ☐

7 Our dog don't have a ball. ☐
Our dog doesn't have a ball. ☐

8 I don't have a laptop. ☐
I doesn't have a laptop. ☐

9 My mom doesn't get up at 7:30am. ☐
My mom don't get up at 7:30am. ☐

10 You doesn't live in the country. ☐
You don't live in the country. ☐

11 Claude don't have a dictionary. ☐
Claude doesn't have a dictionary. ☐

🔊

16.6 LISTEN TO THE AUDIO AND ANSWER THE QUESTIONS

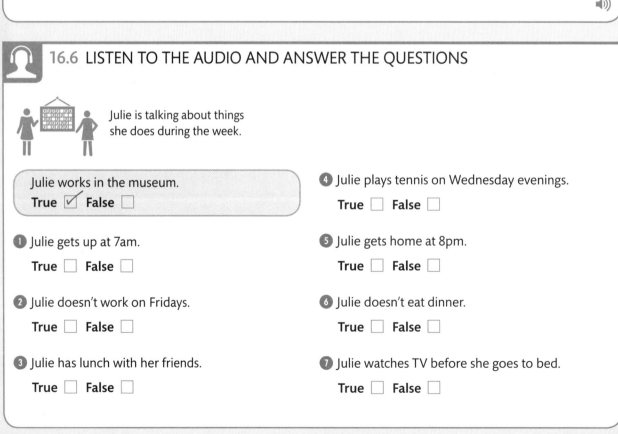

Julie is talking about things she does during the week.

Julie works in the museum.
True ☑ **False** ☐

1 Julie gets up at 7am.
True ☐ **False** ☐

2 Julie doesn't work on Fridays.
True ☐ **False** ☐

3 Julie has lunch with her friends.
True ☐ **False** ☐

4 Julie plays tennis on Wednesday evenings.
True ☐ **False** ☐

5 Julie gets home at 8pm.
True ☐ **False** ☐

6 Julie doesn't eat dinner.
True ☐ **False** ☐

7 Julie watches TV before she goes to bed.
True ☐ **False** ☐

16.7 READ THE ARTICLE AND ANSWER THE QUESTIONS

Who doesn't live in a city?
Sam ☐ **Carla** ☐ **Greg** ☑

1 Who plays a sport on Thursdays?
Sam ☐ **Carla** ☐ **Greg** ☐

2 Who works in the evenings?
Sam ☐ **Carla** ☐ **Greg** ☐

3 Who doesn't have lunch?
Sam ☐ **Carla** ☐ **Greg** ☐

4 Who works in an office?
Sam ☐ **Carla** ☐ **Greg** ☐

5 Who doesn't work on Mondays?
Sam ☐ **Carla** ☐ **Greg** ☐

6 Who starts work at 5am?
Sam ☐ **Carla** ☐ **Greg** ☐

7 Who plays basketball on Mondays?
Sam ☐ **Carla** ☐ **Greg** ☐

8 Who plays soccer?
Sam ☐ **Carla** ☐ **Greg** ☐

What I do

Sam

I'm a waiter from New York. I like my job. I work evenings and the food is fantastic. I work from Tuesday to Sunday, and I don't work on Mondays. On Mondays I play basketball in the afternoon.

Carla

I work in an office in Dublin. I start work at 9am and have lunch at 1pm. I love sports. I play soccer with my colleagues on Thursday evenings.

Greg

I live in the country in South Australia. I work on a farm and start work at 5am. I have a big breakfast and a big dinner, but I don't have lunch. Every weekend, I play golf.

16.8 USE THE CHART TO CREATE NINE CORRECT SENTENCES AND SAY THEM OUT LOUD

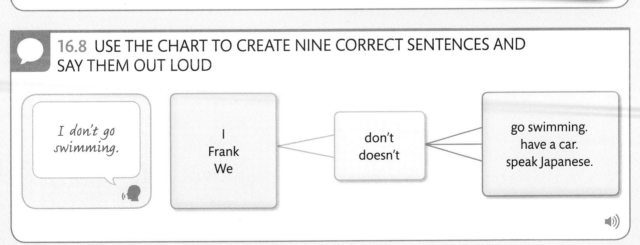

I don't go swimming.

| I Frank We | don't doesn't | go swimming. have a car. speak Japanese. |

53

17 Simple questions

To form simple questions with the verb "to be," you change the order of the subject and verb. The answer to a simple question usually starts with "yes" or "no."

⚙ New language Simple questions
Aa Vocabulary Jobs and routine activities
🧩 New skill Asking simple questions

17.1 REWRITE THE STATEMENTS AS QUESTIONS

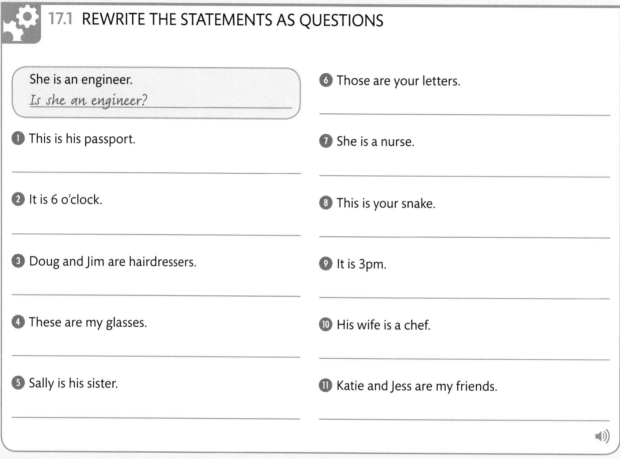

She is an engineer.
Is she an engineer?

① This is his passport.

② It is 6 o'clock.

③ Doug and Jim are hairdressers.

④ These are my glasses.

⑤ Sally is his sister.

⑥ Those are your letters.

⑦ She is a nurse.

⑧ This is your snake.

⑨ It is 3pm.

⑩ His wife is a chef.

⑪ Katie and Jess are my friends.

17.2 USE THE CHART TO CREATE SIX DIFFERENT QUESTIONS AND SAY THEM OUT LOUD

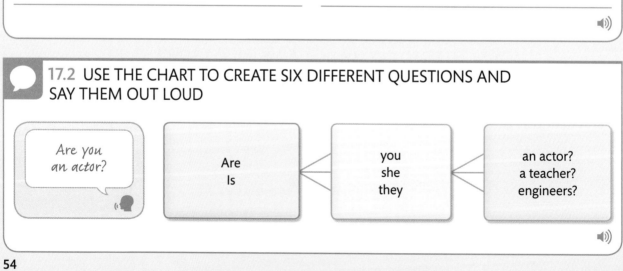

Are you an actor?

| Are / Is | you / she / they | an actor? / a teacher? / engineers? |

17.3 FILL IN THE GAPS USING "IS" OR "ARE"

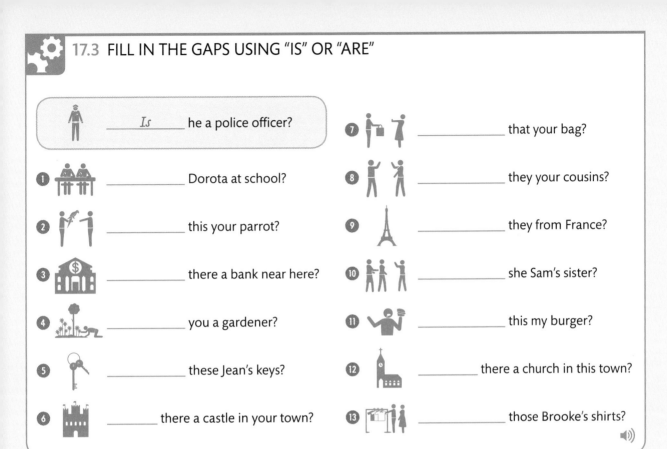

_____Is_____ he a police officer?

1. _____ Dorota at school?

2. _____ this your parrot?

3. _____ there a bank near here?

4. _____ you a gardener?

5. _____ these Jean's keys?

6. _____ there a castle in your town?

7. _____ that your bag?

8. _____ they your cousins?

9. _____ they from France?

10. _____ she Sam's sister?

11. _____ this my burger?

12. _____ there a church in this town?

13. _____ those Brooke's shirts?

17.4 REWRITE THE QUESTIONS, PUTTING THE WORDS IN THE CORRECT ORDER

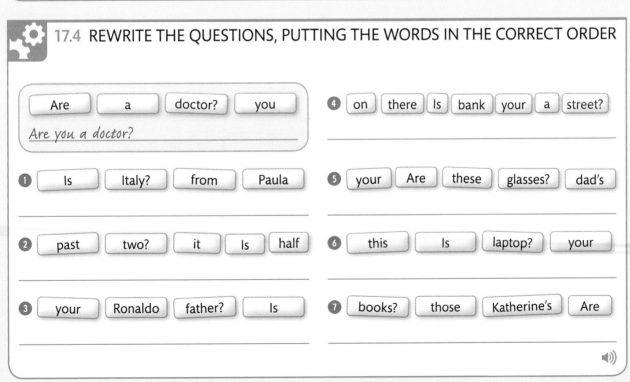

| Are | a | doctor? | you |

Are you a doctor?

1. | Is | Italy? | from | Paula |

_____

2. | past | two? | it | Is | half |

_____

3. | your | Ronaldo | father? | Is |

_____

4. | on | there | Is | bank | your | a | street? |

_____

5. | your | Are | these | glasses? | dad's |

_____

6. | this | Is | laptop? | your |

_____

7. | books? | those | Katherine's | Are |

_____

17.5 FILL IN THE GAPS WITH "DO" OR "DOES"

 Does Maria go swimming?

 1 _____ you work in a hospital?

 2 _____ your dog like children?

 3 _____ you get up at 10am on Sundays?

 4 _____ Simone work with children?

 5 _____ they live in the town?

 6 _____ we finish work at 3pm today?

 7 _____ Frank play tennis with Pete?

17.6 CROSS OUT THE INCORRECT WORD IN EACH QUESTION

Do / ~~Does~~ they play tennis together?

1 Do / Does you read a newspaper every day?

2 Do / Does he go to bed at 11pm?

3 Do / Does they live in a castle?

4 Do / Does Pedro come from Bolivia?

5 Do / Does she work with children?

6 Do / Does Claire and Sam eat lunch at 2pm?

7 Do / Does your brother work with animals?

8 Do / Does Tim play soccer on Mondays?

9 Do / Does they work in a café?

10 Do / Does you have a shower in the evening?

11 Do / Does we start work at 10am on Thursdays?

12 Do / Does Pamela work in a bank?

17.7 REWRITE THE STATEMENTS AS QUESTIONS

Bill gets up at 7am.
Does Bill get up at 7am?

1 They work in a museum.

_____

2 You work with children.

_____

3 Shane lives in Sydney.

_____

4 John plays tennis on Wednesdays.

_____

5 Yves and Marie eat dinner at 6pm.

_____

6 Seth works in a post office.

_____

17.8 READ THE EMAIL AND ANSWER THE QUESTIONS

Does Sam get up at 7:30am?
Yes ☐ No ☑

❶ Does Sam have a bath?
Yes ☐ No ☐

❷ Does he eat breakfast at home?
Yes ☐ No ☐

❸ Does he eat some fruit at work?
Yes ☐ No ☐

❹ Does he work in a bank?
Yes ☐ No ☐

❺ Does Sam's work finish at 6pm?
Yes ☐ No ☐

❻ Does he have lunch at 2:30pm?
Yes ☐ No ☐

❼ Does he watch TV in the evening?
Yes ☐ No ☐

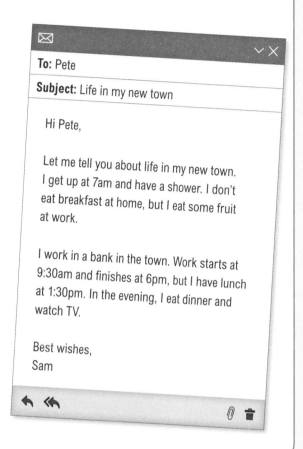

To: Pete

Subject: Life in my new town

Hi Pete,

Let me tell you about life in my new town. I get up at 7am and have a shower. I don't eat breakfast at home, but I eat some fruit at work.

I work in a bank in the town. Work starts at 9:30am and finishes at 6pm, but I have lunch at 1:30pm. In the evening, I eat dinner and watch TV.

Best wishes,
Sam

17.9 SAY THE SENTENCES OUT LOUD, FILLING IN THE GAPS

_Do_ you go to the movies on Saturdays?

❸ _____ Sam and Doug work with animals?

❶ _____ you go to a restaurant on Fridays?

❹ _____ she get up at 7am on the weekend?

❷ _____ Peter live near the museum?

❺ _____ they play tennis in the evening?

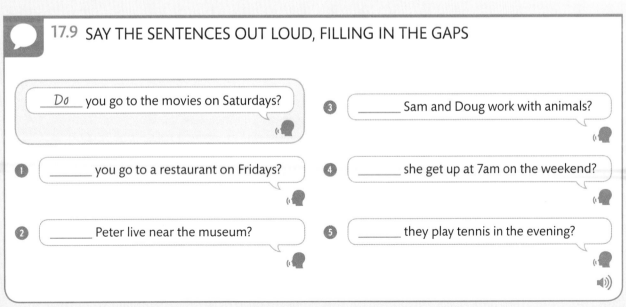

18 Answering questions

When answering questions in English, you can often leave out words to shorten your response. These short answers are often used in spoken English.

⚙ **New language** Simple answers
Aa Vocabulary Jobs and routines
New skill Answering spoken questions

18.1 MARK THE BEST REPLY TO EACH QUESTION

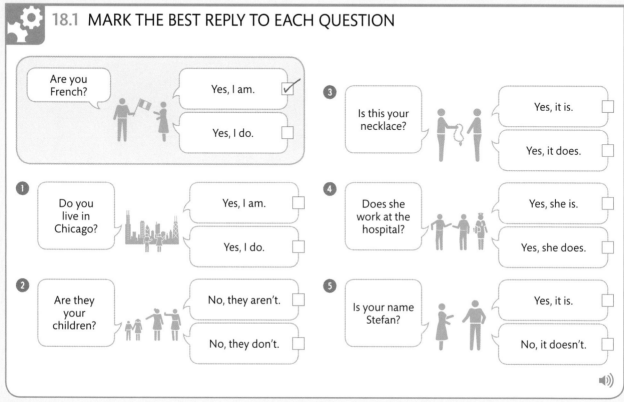

Are you French?
Yes, I am. ✓
Yes, I do. ☐

❶ Do you live in Chicago?
Yes, I am. ☐
Yes, I do. ☐

❷ Are they your children?
No, they aren't. ☐
No, they don't. ☐

❸ Is this your necklace?
Yes, it is. ☐
Yes, it does. ☐

❹ Does she work at the hospital?
Yes, she is. ☐
Yes, she does. ☐

❺ Is your name Stefan?
Yes, it is. ☐
No, it doesn't. ☐

🔊

18.2 FILL IN THE GAPS WITH THE CORRECT SHORT ANSWERS

Is this your cat?
Yes, _it is._

❶ Do you play golf?
No, _____

❷ Is Paula your wife?
Yes, _____

❸ Does Peter speak French?
No, _____

❹ Do they work at the factory?
No, _____

❺ Is Mario from Italy?
Yes, _____

🔊

18.3 READ THE EMAIL AND WRITE ANSWERS TO THE QUESTIONS AS FULL SENTENCES

Does Helen have a new job?

Yes, she does.

❶ Is Helen a German teacher?

_____

❷ Does Helen start work at 8am?

_____

❸ Is Helen's school small?

_____

❹ Does Helen finish at 4pm?

_____

❺ Does Helen read a book in the evening?

_____

✉ ⌄ ✕

To: Kim

Subject: My new job

Hi Kim,

I have some great news! I have a new job. I'm a French teacher at the school on Palm Avenue. Let me tell you about my typical day.

I get up at 8am and I walk to work. The school is big and has 800 children. I start work at 9am and I have lunch at 1pm. My students are very nice! I finish work at 4pm, and then I walk home. In the evening, I mark up my students' homework, then drink a glass of wine and watch a movie.

Say hello to Bob!
Helen

↩ ↩↩   📎 🗑

18.4 LISTEN TO THE AUDIO AND ANSWER THE QUESTIONS

Jane is starting a new job as a teacher. She meets Bob, another teacher at the school.

Jane is a teacher.
True ✓   **False** ☐   **Not given** ☐

❶ Bob is an English teacher.
True ☐   **False** ☐   **Not given** ☐

❷ Jane is from Dublin.
True ☐   **False** ☐   **Not given** ☐

❸ Jane's husband is a teacher too.
True ☐   **False** ☐   **Not given** ☐

❹ Jane's husband works near their house.
True ☐   **False** ☐   **Not given** ☐

❺ Jane's husband starts work at 8:30am.
True ☐   **False** ☐   **Not given** ☐

❻ Bob plays tennis every weekend.
True ☐   **False** ☐   **Not given** ☐

❼ Jane goes to the movies a lot.
True ☐   **False** ☐   **Not given** ☐

19 Asking questions

Use question words such as "what," "who," "when," and "where" to ask open questions that can't be answered with "yes" or "no."

⚙ **New language** Open questions
Aa Vocabulary Question words
🧩 **New skill** Asking for details

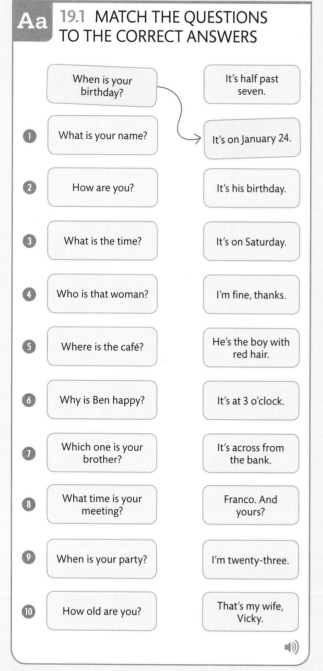

Aa 19.1 MATCH THE QUESTIONS TO THE CORRECT ANSWERS

When is your birthday?	It's half past seven.
❶ What is your name?	It's on January 24.
❷ How are you?	It's his birthday.
❸ What is the time?	It's on Saturday.
❹ Who is that woman?	I'm fine, thanks.
❺ Where is the café?	He's the boy with red hair.
❻ Why is Ben happy?	It's at 3 o'clock.
❼ Which one is your brother?	It's across from the bank.
❽ What time is your meeting?	Franco. And yours?
❾ When is your party?	I'm twenty-three.
❿ How old are you?	That's my wife, Vicky.

🔊

⚙ 19.2 FILL IN THE GAPS TO COMPLETE THE QUESTIONS

_____How_____ old are you?

❶ _____ does the dog keep barking?

❷ _____ are your parents now?

❸ _____ is your brother?

❹ _____ is your name?

❺ _____ is Carla's birthday?

❻ _____ is your sister's house?

❼ _____ car is yours?

❽ _____ are your exams?

❾ _____ did you park the car?

❿ _____ are you sad?

⓫ _____ can I go home?

⓬ _____ does your brother live?

⓭ _____ is your first memory?

Where	When	Where	When
Who	~~How~~	Why	Which	When
What	Where	Why	What	Where

🔊

60

19.3 LISTEN TO THE AUDIO AND ANSWER THE QUESTIONS

Greg is talking about the various members of his family.

What is Greg's grandmother's name?

Shelley ☐

Ellie ☑

Emma ☐

1 How old is Greg's grandmother?

84 years old ☐

82 years old ☐

83 years old ☐

2 Where does she live?

Near the church ☐

Near the cathedral ☐

Near the supermarket ☐

3 Where does Greg's mother work?

At a school ☐

At a museum ☐

At a theater ☐

4 What does Greg's mother do?

She's a cleaner ☐

She's a receptionist ☐

She's a teacher ☐

5 How old is Samantha?

21 ☐

19 ☐

23 ☐

19.4 REWRITE THE SENTENCES, PUTTING THE WORDS IN THE CORRECT ORDER

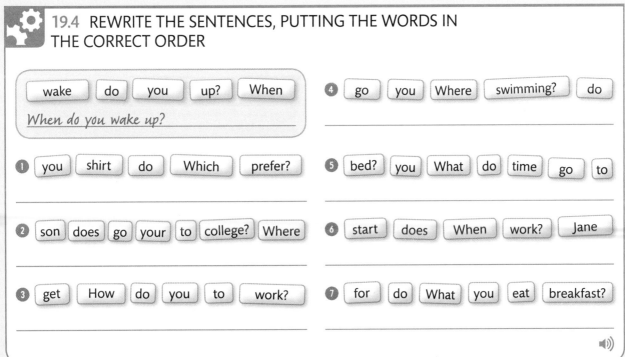

wake | do | you | up? | When

When do you wake up?

1 you | shirt | do | Which | prefer?

_____

2 son | does | go | your | to | college? | Where

_____

3 get | How | do | you | to | work?

_____

4 go | you | Where | swimming? | do

_____

5 bed? | you | What | do | time | go | to

_____

6 start | does | When | work? | Jane

_____

7 for | do | What | you | eat | breakfast?

_____

19.5 SAY THE SENTENCES OUT LOUD, FILLING IN THE GAPS USING THE WORDS IN THE PANEL

_____What_____ do you do?

1 _____ do you study?

2 _____ do you want?

3 _____ building is your college?

4 _____ do you live?

5 _____ time do you wake up?

6 _____ many shirts do you own?

7 _____ do you want for lunch?

8 _____ does the course finish?

9 _____ do you do in the evening?

What   What   Which   ~~What~~   When   How   Which   What   What   Where

19.6 REWRITE THE SENTENCES, CORRECTING THE ERRORS

Where **does** you work?
Where do you work?

1 Which school **do** he go to?

_____

2 Why does Kevin **works** there?

_____

3 Where **do** your friend live?

_____

4 Where **are** your car?

_____

5 What **do** your brother do?

_____

19.7 REWRITE THE SENTENCES AS QUESTIONS

Jerry goes to the movies on Thursdays.
When _does Jerry go to the movies?_

1 My uncle is very well, thanks.

How _____

2 My wife is the woman with long dark hair.

Which _____

3 I work at the school on Sandy Lane.

Where _____

4 The meeting is at 3:30pm.

What _____

5 I finish work at 7pm tonight.

When _____

19.8 USE THE CHART TO CREATE 12 CORRECT SENTENCES AND SAY THEM OUT LOUD

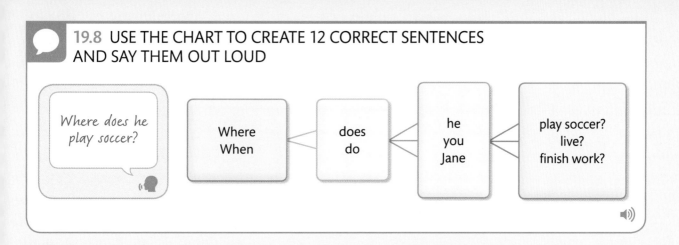

Where does he play soccer?

| Where / When | does / do | he / you / Jane | play soccer? / live? / finish work? |

19.9 READ THE EMAIL AND ANSWER THE QUESTIONS

Which country are Tim and Janet in?
France ✓ **Italy** ☐

1 What is the name of the town?
Blois ☐ **Tours** ☐

2 Who is Tim with?
Janet ☐ **Claire** ☐

3 Where is their hotel?
Near the castle ☐ **Near the cathedral** ☐

4 What do they eat for breakfast?
Cereal ☐ **French bread** ☐

5 Where do they drink their coffee?
In the hotel ☐ **In a café** ☐

6 What do they do in the afternoon?
Explore the old town ☐ **Visit a restaurant** ☐

7 How old is the castle?
About 200 years old ☐ **About 1,000 years old** ☐

8 What can you see at the castle?
Some beautiful paintings ☐ **Historic furniture** ☐

✉

To: Claire

Subject: Having fun!

Hello Claire,

We're on vacation in France this week! We're in Blois, a small town near Tours. I am here with Janet, an old friend from school. Our hotel is near the castle in the old town, and is not far from some nice cafés and restaurants. We eat French bread for breakfast every morning, and I buy it from a local bakery. In the morning, Janet and I go for coffee in a local café and eat a pastry. French pastries are delicious. In the afternoon, we walk by the river and explore the old town. There are some excellent stores, so I'll get you a present. The castle is amazing. It's about 1,000 years old and has lots of rooms with beautiful paintings.

See you soon!
Tim

20 Vocabulary

Aa 20.1 AROUND TOWN WRITE THE WORDS FROM THE PANEL UNDER THE CORRECT PICTURES

village

① _____

② _____

③ _____

④ _____

⑦ _____

⑧ _____

⑨ _____

⑩ _____

⑪ _____

⑭ _____

⑮ _____

⑯ _____

⑰ _____

⑱ _____

㉑ _____

㉒ _____

㉓ _____

㉔ _____

㉕ _____

5 _____

6 _____

12 _____

13 _____

19 _____

20 _____

26 _____

27 _____

supermarket   pharmacy

far   hospital   bus station

library   café   post office

here   ~~village~~   town

park   castle   airport

police station   there   bank

bridge   factory   bar

mosque   train station   near

hotel   school   office building

swimming pool   restaurant

🔊

21 Talking about your town

When you talk about things, you can use "there is" for one and "there are" for more than one. "There isn't" and "there aren't" are the negatives.

New language There is / There are
Aa Vocabulary Town and buildings
New skill Describe a town

21.1 FILL IN THE GAPS TO COMPLETE THE SENTENCES

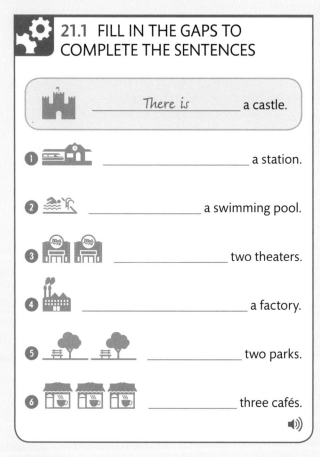

_____There is_____ a castle.

① _____ a station.

② _____ a swimming pool.

③ _____ two theaters.

④ _____ a factory.

⑤ _____ two parks.

⑥ _____ three cafés.

21.2 CROSS OUT THE INCORRECT WORDS IN EACH SENTENCE

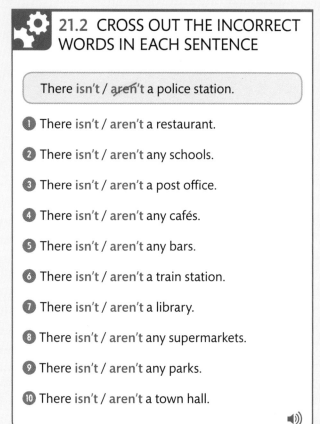

There isn't / aren't a police station.

① There isn't / aren't a restaurant.

② There isn't / aren't any schools.

③ There isn't / aren't a post office.

④ There isn't / aren't any cafés.

⑤ There isn't / aren't any bars.

⑥ There isn't / aren't a train station.

⑦ There isn't / aren't a library.

⑧ There isn't / aren't any supermarkets.

⑨ There isn't / aren't any parks.

⑩ There isn't / aren't a town hall.

21.3 SAY EIGHT CORRECT SENTENCES USING THE WORDS IN THE CHART

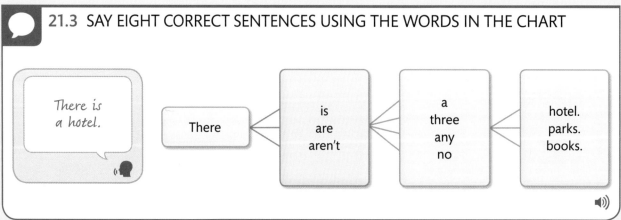

There is a hotel.

| There | is / are / aren't | a / three / any / no | hotel. / parks. / books. |

21.4 LISTEN TO THE AUDIO AND NUMBER THE PICTURES IN THE ORDER THEY ARE DESCRIBED

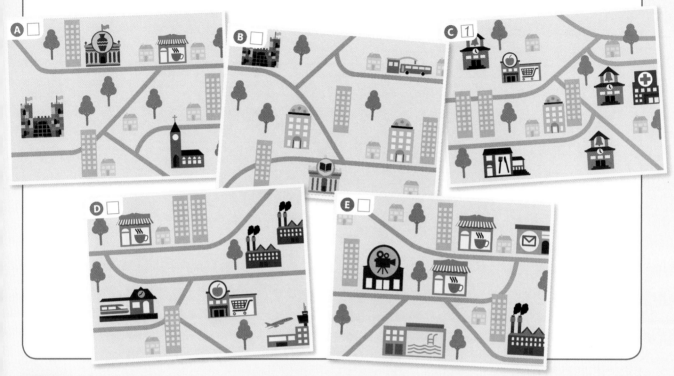

21.5 REWRITE EACH SENTENCE IN THE NEGATIVE FORM

There is a theater.	=	*There isn't a theater.*
❶ There is a school.	=	
❷ There are two churches.	=	
❸ There is a café.	=	
❹ There is a library.	=	
❺ There are two airports.	=	
❻ There are three hotels.	=	
❼ There are two parks.	=	
❽ There is a town hall.	=	

21.6 LISTEN TO THE AUDIO AND MARK THE CORRECT ANSWERS

Gordon is describing the town he lives in with his family.

Melcome is in...
Scotland. ☐
Canada. ☑
England. ☐
New Zealand. ☐

❶ There are two ...... in Melcome.
post offices ☐
banks ☐
churches ☐
offices ☐

❷ Gordon works in a...
museum. ☐
café. ☐
factory. ☐
primary school. ☐

❸ In the evening Gordon goes to a...
library. ☐
café. ☐
restaurant. ☐
swimming pool. ☐

❹ Gordon's wife works in a...
hospital. ☐
theater. ☐
store. ☐
post office. ☐

❺ Gordon's son is a...
teacher. ☐
doctor. ☐
police officer. ☐
actor. ☐

21.7 REWRITE THE SENTENCES PUTTING THE WORDS IN THE CORRECT ORDER

| are | three | cafés. | There |

There are three cafés.

❶ | supermarket. | is | a | There |

_____

❷ | restaurants. | There | any | aren't |

_____

❸ | hotels. | are | There | no |

_____

❹ | There | three | are | schools. |

_____

❺ | is | station. | a | There | bus |

_____

21.8 READ THE EMAIL AND ANSWER THE QUESTIONS

There are two beaches.
True ☐ **False** ☑

1 There isn't a castle.
True ☐ **False** ☐

2 There is a park.
True ☐ **False** ☐

3 There is a supermarket.
True ☐ **False** ☐

4 There aren't any stores.
True ☐ **False** ☐

5 There is a big restaurant.
True ☐ **False** ☐

6 There are four cafés.
True ☐ **False** ☐

7 There is an airport.
True ☐ **False** ☐

✉   ⌄ ✕

To: Christine

Subject: Visiting Westport

Hi Christine,
We are on vacation in Westport and it's beautiful! There's lots
to do here for all the family. There aren't any beaches, but
there's a castle and a big park. The castle is very old and really
interesting. And the children go to the park every day. There
isn't a supermarket here, but there are lots of small stores in
the center. Anne loves them.
In the evening, I walk with Anne and the children in the center.
There is a big fish restaurant here. I like fish a lot! There are
also three cafés where we relax. It's easy to get to Westport.
The airport is not far from the center and there's a bus station
near our hotel.

Wish you were here!
See you soon!
Tom

↩ ↩↩   🖉 🗑

21.9 LOOK AT THE IMAGE AND SAY THE SENTENCES OUT LOUD, FILLING IN THE GAPS

___There is___ a library. 🗣

1 _____ stores. 🗣

2 _____ castles. 🗣

3 _____ a church. 🗣

4 _____ a hospital. 🗣

5 _____ a post office. 🗣

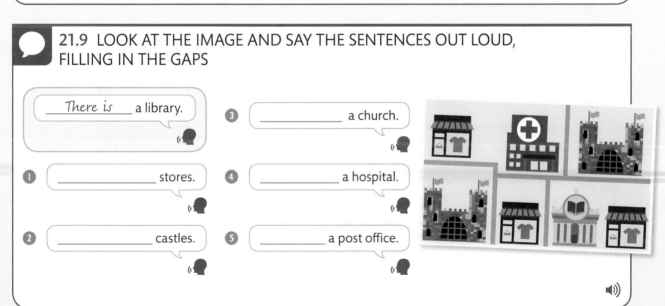

🔊

22 Using "a" and "the"

Use the definite article ("the") or indefinite article ("a," "an") to talk about things in specific or general terms. Use "some" to talk about more than one thing.

⚙ **New language** Definite and indefinite articles
Aa Vocabulary Places in town
🧩 **New skill** Using articles

22.1 CROSS OUT THE INCORRECT WORDS IN EACH SENTENCE

Alex is a / ~~an~~ / ~~the~~ teacher.

1 A / An / The new doctor is called Hilary.

2 Sammy is a / an / the nurse.

3 There is a / an / the bank downtown.

4 Is there a / an / the hospital near here?

5 A / An / The gym is near Sam's house.

6 There is a / an / the new café in town.

7 A / An / The hotel on Elm Lane is nice.

8 A / An / The new teacher is good.

9 There's a / an / the old theater in town.

🔊

22.2 REWRITE THE SENTENCES CORRECTING THE ERRORS

A new teacher is called Mr. Smith.
The new teacher is called Mr. Smith.

1 I have the sister and the brother.

_____

2 There is the library on Queens Road.

_____

3 I bought a apple and a orange.

_____

4 Is there the bank near here?

_____

5 There is an café at the bus station.

_____

6 My dad is a engineer.

_____

7 There is the cell phone on the table.

_____

🔊

22.3 FILL IN THE GAPS USING "A," "AN," "SOME," OR "THE"

Dear Bob and Sally,

We are in Glenmuir, ——— quiet town in Scotland. There's ——— castle and ——— cathedral here. They're beautiful and ——— castle is really old. There are ——— interesting stores, which we visit every day. We also have ——— new friend here. He's called Alfonso and he works as ——— waiter in ——— Italian restaurant next to ——— shopping mall. He's great!

Jane

 22.4 CROSS OUT THE INCORRECT WORDS IN EACH SENTENCE

Is there a / an / any museum in Littleton?

1 Are there a / an / any factories in your town?

2 Is there a / an / any gym downtown?

3 Are there a / an / any pencils in your bag?

4 Is there a / an / any old church on Station Road?

5 Is there a / an / any hospital in the town?

6 Is there a / an / any salon near here?

7 Is there a / an / any apple in the basket?

8 Are there a / an / any restaurants in your town?

9 Is there a / an / any library downtown?

10 Are there a / an / any books on the table?

11 Is there a / an / any café nearby?

12 Is there a / an / any cathedral in that town?

13 Is there a / an / any bank near the supermarket?

14 Are there a / an / any kittens here?

15 Is there a / an / any school in this neighborhood?

22.5 REWRITE THE SENTENCES PUTTING THE WORDS IN THE CORRECT ORDER

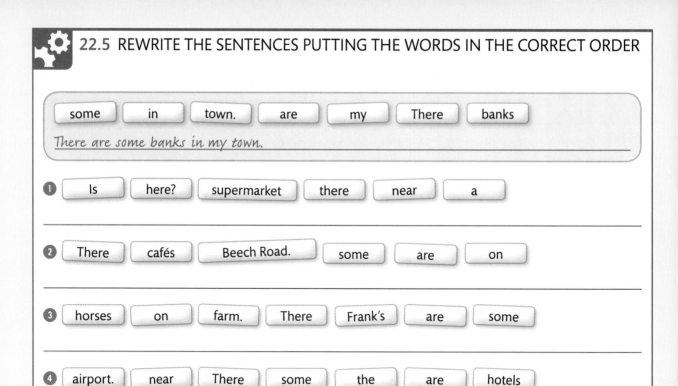

some | in | town. | are | my | There | banks

There are some banks in my town.

① Is | here? | supermarket | there | near | a

_____

② There | cafés | Beech Road. | some | are | on

_____

③ horses | on | farm. | There | Frank's | are | some

_____

④ airport. | near | There | some | the | are | hotels

_____

22.6 SAY THE SENTENCES OUT LOUD, FILLING IN THE GAPS

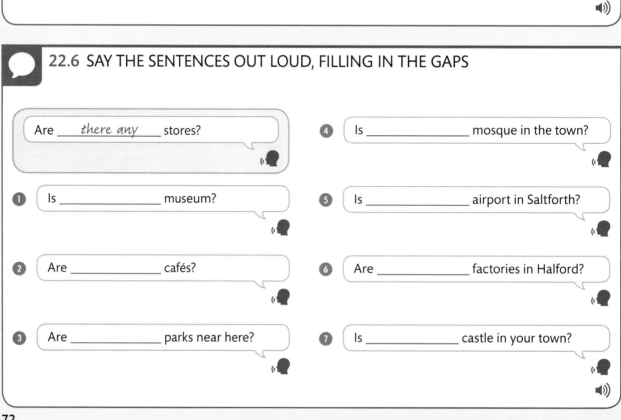

Are _____ _there any_ _____ stores?

① Is _____ museum?

② Are _____ cafés?

③ Are _____ parks near here?

④ Is _____ mosque in the town?

⑤ Is _____ airport in Saltforth?

⑥ Are _____ factories in Halford?

⑦ Is _____ castle in your town?

22.7 RESPOND OUT LOUD TO THE AUDIO, FILLING IN THE GAPS

Are there any cinemas in Littleton?

No, _____*there aren't.*_____

④ Is there a park in your town?

No, _____

① Are there any supermarkets in the town?

Yes, _____

⑤ Is there a good restaurant near the park?

Yes, _____

② Is there a church on Duke Road?

No, _____

⑥ Are there any castles near your town?

No, _____

③ Are there any theaters near the hotel?

Yes, _____

⑦ Are there any bars and cafés downtown?

Yes, _____

22.8 LISTEN TO THE AUDIO AND ANSWER THE QUESTIONS

James is describing his life on a farm.

Where does James live?
on a farm ☑   in a city ☐   in a town ☐

④ What restaurant does Stonehill have?
Italian ☐   French ☐   Mexican ☐

① Where is the museum?
Stonehill ☐   Eastford ☐   There isn't one ☐

⑤ Are there any theaters in Stonehill?
some ☐   none ☐   lots ☐

② Where does James go on the weekend?
theater ☐   church ☐   museum ☐

⑥ How many churches are there in Eastford?
two ☐   four ☐   six ☐

③ Are there any stores in Stonehill?
some ☐   none ☐   lots ☐

⑦ Are there any stores in Eastford?
some ☐   none ☐   lots ☐

23 Orders and directions

Use imperatives to tell someone to do something. They are also useful to give a warning, or to give directions to someone.

⚙ **New language** Imperatives
Aa Vocabulary Directions
✎ **New skill** Finding your way

23.1 REWRITE EACH VERB AS AN IMPERATIVE

he takes = _take_

① to put = _____

② I read = _____

③ she works = _____

④ to start = _____

⑤ you eat = _____

⑥ they have = _____

⑦ it stops = _____

⑧ to wake up = _____

⑨ we run = _____

⑩ they come = _____

⑪ you are = _____

🔊

23.2 MARK WHETHER EACH SENTENCE IS IMPERATIVE OR PRESENT SIMPLE

Eat your breakfast.
imperative ☑   present simple ☐

① I eat my dinner at 6pm.
imperative ☐   present simple ☐

② Come with me.
imperative ☐   present simple ☐

③ You read your book every day.
imperative ☐   present simple ☐

④ Give that to me.
imperative ☐   present simple ☐

⑤ Read this book.
imperative ☐   present simple ☐

⑥ Eat your dinner.
imperative ☐   present simple ☐

⑦ She goes to bed at 9pm.
imperative ☐   present simple ☐

⑧ I start school at 9am.
imperative ☐   present simple ☐

⑨ Go to bed.
imperative ☐   present simple ☐

🔊

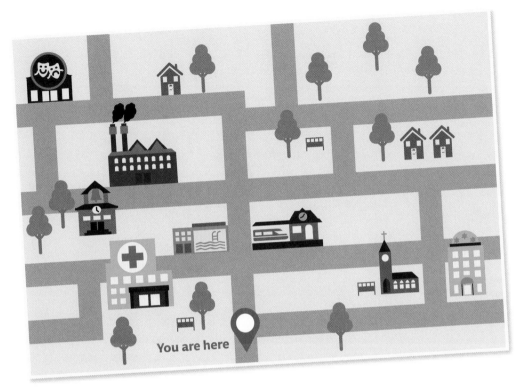

For the hospital...
Take the first left. The hospital is on the left ☑
Take the first left. The hospital is on the right. ☐

1 For the swimming pool...
Go straight ahead. The swimming pool is opposite the castle. ☐
Go straight ahead. The swimming pool is opposite the station. ☐

2 For the school...
Take the second left. The school is opposite the factory. ☐
Take the third left. The school is next to the factory. ☐

3 For the church...
Turn right and take the second right. The church is opposite the hotel. ☐
Turn right and take the first left. The church is opposite the hotel. ☐

4 For the theater...
Take the third left and go straight ahead. The theater is on the right. ☐
Take the third right and go straight ahead. The theater is on the left. ☐

🔊

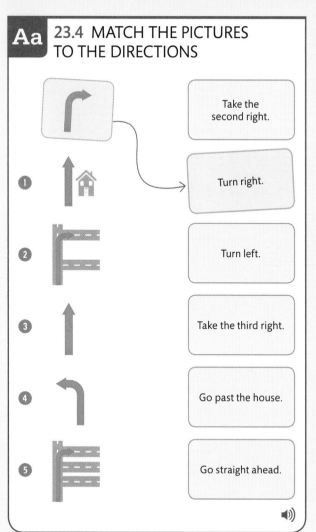

Aa 23.4 MATCH THE PICTURES TO THE DIRECTIONS

Take the second right.

① Turn right.

Turn left.

② Take the third right.

③

④ Go past the house.

⑤ Go straight ahead.

🔊

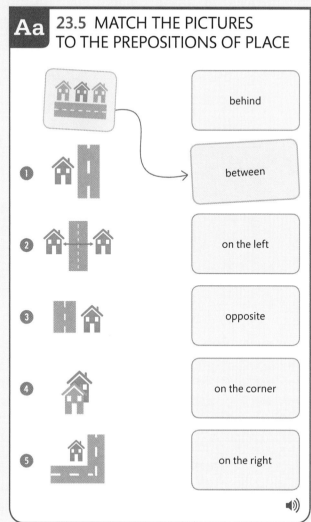

Aa 23.5 MATCH THE PICTURES TO THE PREPOSITIONS OF PLACE

behind

① between

② on the left

③ opposite

④ on the corner

⑤ on the right

🔊

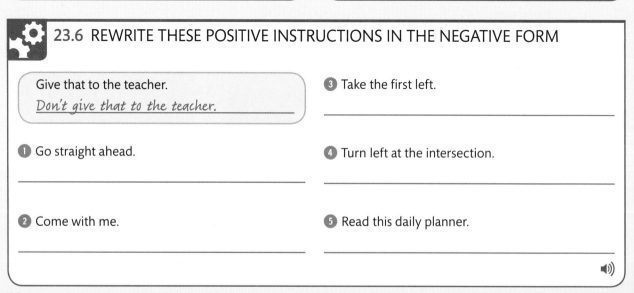

23.6 REWRITE THESE POSITIVE INSTRUCTIONS IN THE NEGATIVE FORM

Give that to the teacher.
Don't give that to the teacher.

① Go straight ahead.

② Come with me.

③ Take the first left.

④ Turn left at the intersection.

⑤ Read this daily planner.

🔊

23.7 LISTEN TO THE AUDIO AND NUMBER THE DIRECTIONS IN THE ORDER YOU HEAR THEM

Turn left and the theater is on your right across from the church. | 1 |

A The café is on the corner next to the church. ☐

B The restaurant is on the right next to the bank. ☐

C Go straight ahead and take the second road on your right. ☐

D Turn right, then take the first left. ☐

E Go past the hotel and the café is on the left. ☐

F The hospital is on the corner on the left. ☐

G Go straight ahead and it's the fourth road on the right. ☐

H Go straight ahead and take the third left. ☐

Aa 23.8 LOOK AT THE PICTURES AND USE PREPOSITIONS TO COMPLETE THE SENTENCES

The supermarket is

_____next to_____ the hotel.

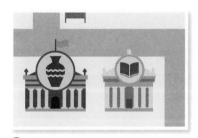

1 The museum is

_____ the library.

2 The restaurant is

_____ the store.

3 The hospital is

_____ the theater.

4 The post office is

_____ the school.

in front of	behind
~~next to~~	
opposite	next to

🔊

77

24 Joining sentences

"And" and "but" are conjunctions: words that join statements together. "And" adds things to a sentence or links sentences together. "But" introduces a contrast to a sentence.

New language Using "and" and "but"
Aa Vocabulary Town, jobs, and family
New skill Joining sentences

Aa 24.1 MATCH THE BEGINNINGS OF THE SENTENCES TO THE CORRECT ENDINGS

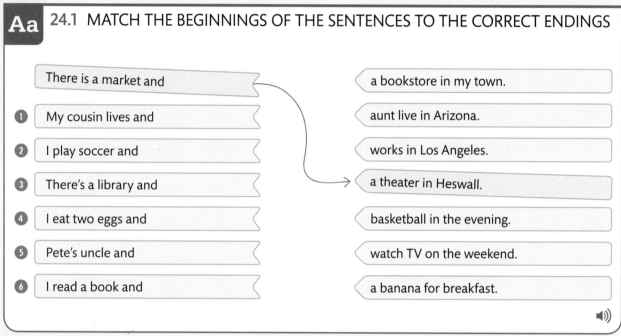

There is a market and ——————→ a theater in Heswall.

a bookstore in my town.

1. My cousin lives and
aunt live in Arizona.

2. I play soccer and
works in Los Angeles.

3. There's a library and
a theater in Heswall.

4. I eat two eggs and
basketball in the evening.

5. Pete's uncle and
watch TV on the weekend.

6. I read a book and
a banana for breakfast.

24.2 LISTEN TO THE AUDIO AND MATCH THE TWO PLACES THAT THE SPEAKER DESCRIBES

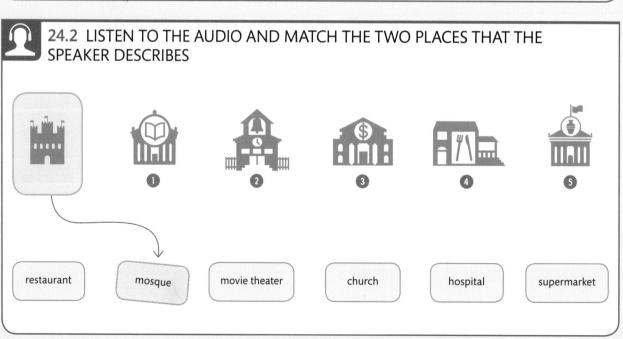

restaurant   mosque   movie theater   church   hospital   supermarket

Aa 24.3 MARK THE SENTENCES THAT ARE CORRECT

There's a library, a store, and a museum. ☑
There's a library, and a store, a museum. ☐

1 Three chefs, four waiters work in my hotel. ☐
Three chefs and four waiters work in my hotel. ☐

2 There's a park, a café, and a theater in Pella. ☐
There's a park, a café, a theater in Pella. ☐

3 I have one aunt, and two sisters, and a niece. ☐
I have one aunt, two sisters, and a niece. ☐

4 Ben eats breakfast, and lunch and dinner. ☐
Ben eats breakfast, lunch, and dinner. ☐

5 I play and tennis and soccer. ☐
I play tennis and soccer. ☐

6 We have and dog and a cat. ☐
We have a dog and a cat. ☐

7 I read a book, take a bath on Sundays. ☐
I read a book and take a bath on Sundays. ☐

8 Jen speaks French, Spanish, Japanese. ☐
Jen speaks French, Spanish, and Japanese. ☐

9 Pete has two dogs and a cat. ☐
Pete has two dogs, a cat. ☐

🔊

⚙ 24.4 REWRITE THE SENTENCES TO JOIN THEM TOGETHER USING "AND" OR "BUT"

I get up. I take a shower.
I get up and take a shower.

1 This is my brother. These are my sisters.
_____

2 I speak English. I don't speak French.
_____

3 I play video games. I watch TV.
_____

4 I have one uncle. I don't have any aunts.
_____

5 There are two stores. There are three hotels.
_____

6 I eat lunch every day. I don't eat breakfast.
_____

7 There's a hotel. There isn't a store.
_____

8 I have a sandwich. I have an apple.
_____

9 This is my house. These aren't my keys.
_____

10 Those are Sarah's magazines. That is her ID card.
_____

11 This phone is Joe's. This laptop isn't Joe's.
_____

🔊

24.5 CROSS OUT THE INCORRECT WORD IN EACH SENTENCE

I work every weekday ~~and~~ / but not on weekends.

1 There's a library, a store, and / but a café.

2 There's a castle and a church and / but there isn't a museum.

3 Pete eats apples and / but doesn't eat bananas.

4 Greg reads magazines and / but a newspaper.

5 I have a calendar and / but a notebook.

6 He goes swimming and / but he doesn't play soccer.

24.6 SAY THE SENTENCES OUT LOUD, FILLING IN THE GAPS

My mom _____ *and* _____ dad work as doctors in the hospital.

1 Meg likes this restaurant _____ she doesn't like that café.

2 There are two schools _____ there isn't a library in my town.

3 I have a pen, a notebook, _____ a calendar in my bag.

4 My sister goes to the gym on Mondays _____ Thursdays.

5 Pedro works in a school _____ he isn't a teacher.

25 Describing places

Use adjectives to give more information about nouns, for example to describe a person, building, or place.

New language Adjectives
Aa Vocabulary Place adjectives and nouns
New skill Describing places

25.1 REWRITE THE SENTENCES, PUTTING THE WORDS IN THE CORRECT ORDER

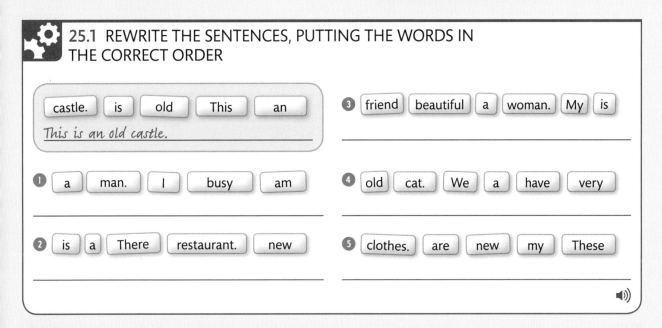

| castle. | is | old | This | an |

This is an old castle.

1 | a | man. | I | busy | am |

_____

2 | is | a | There | restaurant. | new |

_____

3 | friend | beautiful | a | woman. | My | is |

_____

4 | old | cat. | We | a | have | very |

_____

5 | clothes. | are | new | my | These |

_____

25.2 FIND EIGHT ADJECTIVES IN THE EMAIL AND WRITE THEM OUT

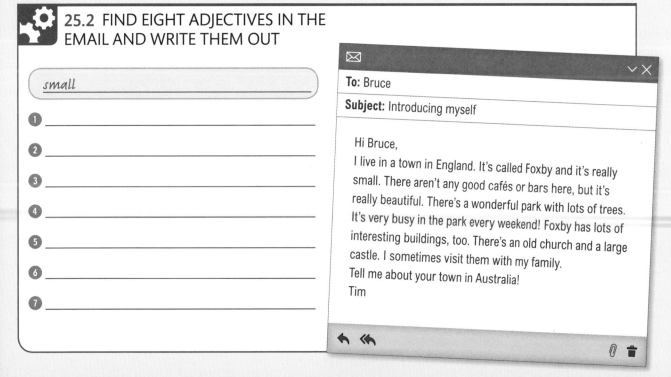

small

1 _____

2 _____

3 _____

4 _____

5 _____

6 _____

7 _____

To: Bruce

Subject: Introducing myself

Hi Bruce,
I live in a town in England. It's called Foxby and it's really small. There aren't any good cafés or bars here, but it's really beautiful. There's a wonderful park with lots of trees. It's very busy in the park every weekend! Foxby has lots of interesting buildings, too. There's an old church and a large castle. I sometimes visit them with my family.
Tell me about your town in Australia!
Tim

25.3 FILL IN THE GAPS TO WRITE EACH SENTENCE IN TWO DIFFERENT WAYS

Paris is a beautiful city.   _The city is beautiful._   _It is beautiful._

1. They are small children. _____ _____

2. Peter is a good waiter. _____ _____

3. Fido is a big dog. _____ _____

4. Melby is a quiet town. _____ _____

Aa 25.4 MATCH THE ADJECTIVES TO THEIR OPPOSITES

busy → quiet

1. old — old
2. small — bad
3. good — old
4. horrible — slow
5. young — large
6. fast — beautiful
7. difficult — new

easy

25.5 LISTEN TO THE AUDIO AND ANSWER THE QUESTIONS

Braemore is a large town in Scotland.
True ☐ **False** ☐ **Not given** ☑

1. There are lots of lakes near Braemore.
True ☐ **False** ☐ **Not given** ☐

2. There are a few old buildings.
True ☐ **False** ☐ **Not given** ☐

3. Braemore has only a few hotels.
True ☐ **False** ☐ **Not given** ☐

4. Kirsty works in a large hotel.
True ☐ **False** ☐ **Not given** ☐

5. Kirsty is not very busy on weekends.
True ☐ **False** ☐ **Not given** ☐

6. Kirsty goes to a café with her friends.
True ☐ **False** ☐ **Not given** ☐

25.6 SAY THE SENTENCES OUT LOUD, FILLING IN THE GAPS

The lakes _are_ beautiful _and the_ beaches _are_ quiet.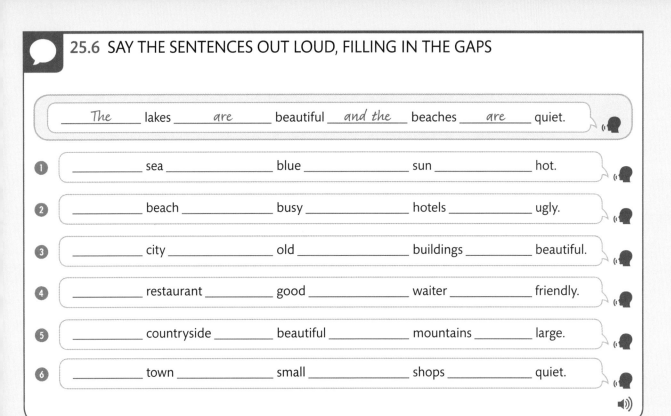

1 _____ sea _____ blue _____ sun _____ hot.

2 _____ beach _____ busy _____ hotels _____ ugly.

3 _____ city _____ old _____ buildings _____ beautiful.

4 _____ restaurant _____ good _____ waiter _____ friendly.

5 _____ countryside _____ beautiful _____ mountains _____ large.

6 _____ town _____ small _____ shops _____ quiet.

Aa 25.7 FILL IN THE GAPS USING THE WORDS IN THE PANEL

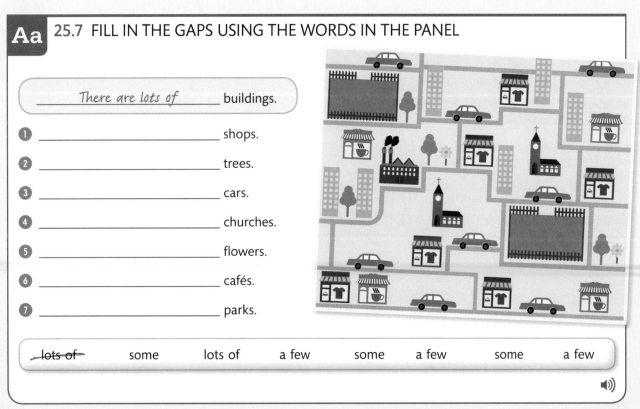

There are lots of buildings.

1 _____ shops.

2 _____ trees.

3 _____ cars.

4 _____ churches.

5 _____ flowers.

6 _____ cafés.

7 _____ parks.

~~lots of~~   some   lots of   a few   some   a few   some   a few

83

26 Giving reasons

Use the conjunction "because" to give a reason for something. You can also use "because" to answer the question "Why?"

⚙ **New language** "Because"
Aa Vocabulary Places and jobs
🧩 **New skill** Giving reasons

Aa 26.1 MATCH THE BEGINNINGS OF THE SENTENCES TO THE CORRECT ENDINGS

I work at night because ─────────────────→ I'm a night nurse.

he's a teacher.

1. Fred works outside because   she's a student.

2. Mick travels to Switzerland because   I'm a mailman.

3. Saul goes to bed late because   I'm a night nurse.

4. I get up at 5am because   he goes skiing there.

5. Marion goes to the library because   he works in a restaurant.

6. Colin works with children because   he's a farmer.

🔊

🎧 26.2 LISTEN TO THE AUDIO AND ANSWER THE QUESTIONS

Leo uses a computer because...
he works in an office ☑ **he works on a farm** ☐

1. Rick works outside because...
   he's a gardener ☐ **he's a farmer** ☐

2. Mary Lou works with children because...
   she's a teacher ☐ **she's a nurse** ☐

3. Carl goes to the library because...
   he's a student ☐ **he's a professor** ☐

4. Sally gets up at 6am because...
   she goes running ☐ **she goes to the gym** ☐

5. Pete works at the theater because...
   he's an actor ☐ **he's a receptionist** ☐

6. Michael has not come to work because...
   he's out of town ☐ **he has the flu** ☐

7. Sana works in a restaurant because...
   she's a chef ☐ **she's a waitress** ☐

26.3 FILL IN THE GAPS USING THE PHRASES IN THE PANEL

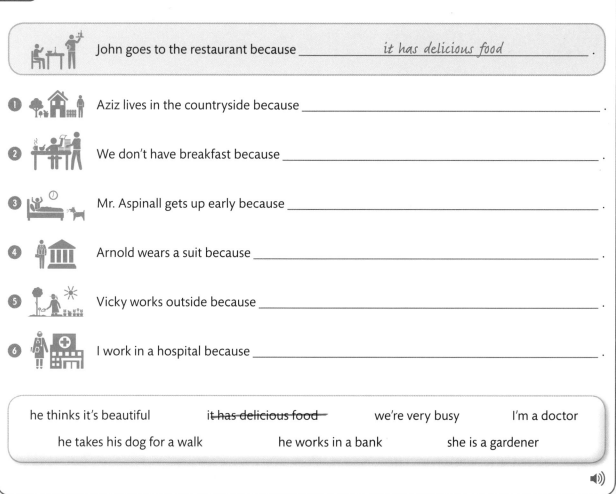

John goes to the restaurant because _____ *it has delicious food* _____ .

1. Aziz lives in the countryside because _____ .

2. We don't have breakfast because _____ .

3. Mr. Aspinall gets up early because _____ .

4. Arnold wears a suit because _____ .

5. Vicky works outside because _____ .

6. I work in a hospital because _____ .

he thinks it's beautiful   ~~it has delicious food~~   we're very busy   I'm a doctor

he takes his dog for a walk   he works in a bank   she is a gardener

26.4 USE THE CHART TO CREATE SIX CORRECT SENTENCES AND SAY THEM OUT LOUD

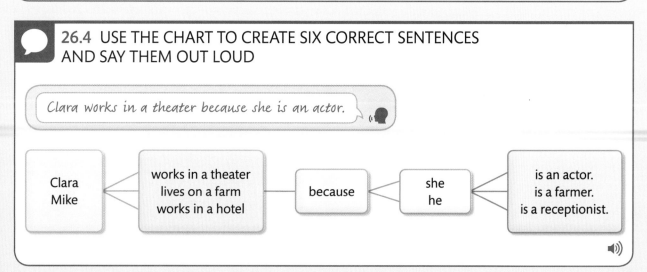

Clara works in a theater because she is an actor.

| Clara Mike | works in a theater lives on a farm works in a hotel | because | she he | is an actor. is a farmer. is a receptionist. |

Aa 27.1 **AROUND THE HOUSE** WRITE THE WORDS FROM THE PANEL UNDER THE CORRECT PICTURES

desk

1 _____

2 _____

3 _____

8 _____

9 _____

10 _____

11 _____

16 _____

17 _____

18 _____

19 _____

---

couch (US) / sofa (UK)   dining room   toilet   house   closet (US) / wardrobe (UK)

bathroom   bedroom   ~~desk~~   chair   bathtub   table   bookcase

④ _____

⑤ _____

⑥ _____

⑦ _____

⑫ _____

⑬ _____

⑭ _____

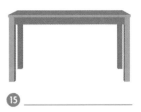

⑮ _____

⑳ _____

㉑ _____

㉒ _____

㉓ _____

kitchen   door   armchair   study   garage   apartment block (US) / block of flats (UK)

lamp   television   bed   shower   window   refrigerator (US) / fridge (UK)

28 The things I have

When you talk about things you own, such as furniture or pets, you can use the verb "have." You can also use it to talk about your qualifications and the appliances and rooms in your home.

⚙ **New language** Using "have"
Aa Vocabulary Household objects
🧩 **New skill** Talking about possessions

⚙ 28.1 CROSS OUT THE INCORRECT WORD IN EACH SENTENCE

 We have / ~~has~~ a car in the garage.

1. My friend **have / has** new glasses.

2. John **have / has** two dogs.

3. We **have / has** an old castle in our city.

4. They **have / has** a lot of parks in their town.

5. I **have / has** a beautiful necklace.

6. Alex **have / has** a new camera.

7. Our house **have / has** a lovely yard.

8. Phil and Sue **have / has** four daughters.

9. Pete **have / has** a new cell phone.

10. Your town **have / has** a big hotel.

11. I **have / has** a lot of friends.

🔊

⚙ 28.2 FILL IN THE GAPS USING "HAS" OR "HAVE"

They __*have*__ two daughters.

1. Bob and Shirley _____ a big dog.

2. She _____ some new friends.

3. We _____ two sons at home.

4. James _____ two cars.

5. His house _____ three bedrooms.

6. Pam _____ lots of books at home.

7. He _____ two cats.

8. Sally's house _____ a new kitchen.

9. You _____ a beautiful house.

10. I _____ three sisters.

11. Kelly and Mark _____ a microwave.

12. We _____ a castle in our town.

13. Sanjay _____ a cat and a dog.

14. You _____ three brothers.

15. Ross _____ a new cell phone.

16. Our house _____ two bathrooms.

17. I _____ a couch in my room.

18. Washington _____ some lovely parks.

🔊

28.3 MARK THE SENTENCES THAT ARE CORRECT

We have apples and oranges. ☑
We apples and oranges have. ☐

1 I have two sisters. ☐
I has two sisters. ☐

2 You has a beautiful house. ☐
You have a beautiful house. ☐

3 We a garden have. ☐
We have a garden. ☐

4 Sam and Greg have a dog. ☐
Sam and Greg has a dog. ☐

5 Marlon a brother has. ☐
Marlon has a brother. ☐

6 Fardale have an old castle. ☐
Fardale has an old castle. ☐

7 They have a new car. ☐
They has a new car. ☐

🔊

28.4 READ THE ADVERTISEMENTS AND ANSWER THE QUESTIONS

Ocean View has two bedrooms.
True ☐ **False** ☑

1 Ocean View has a garage.
True ☐ **False** ☐

2 Sunny Bank has two bathrooms.
True ☐ **False** ☐

3 There isn't a garage at Sunny Bank.
True ☐ **False** ☐

4 Belle Vue Manor has six bedrooms.
True ☐ **False** ☐

5 Belle Vue Manor has a small yard.
True ☐ **False** ☐

6 Mossfield Cottage has an old kitchen.
True ☐ **False** ☐

7 Mossfield Cottage has a small yard.
True ☐ **False** ☐

PROPERTY

Ocean View $2,000/month
This beautiful house is right on the ocean. There are three bedrooms and a big kitchen. It also has a lovely yard, but there is no garage.

Sunny Bank $1,500/month
This modern apartment has two bedrooms and one bathroom with a bath and a shower. All the furniture is new. There isn't a yard, but there is a garage.

Belle Vue Manor
This large house is in the center of Sunset Cove. It has six bedrooms, three bathrooms, and two garages. There is a big yard with lots of trees and a lake.

Mossfield Cottage $1300/month
This small house is in the old part of Summerwood. It has two bedrooms, a bathroom, and a new kitchen. There is a small yard with lots of beautiful flowers.

89

28.5 REWRITE THE STATEMENTS USING CONTRACTIONS

Sam **does not** have a car.
Sam doesn't have a car.

1 We **do not** have a computer at home.

_____

2 My city **does not** have a castle.

_____

3 Rob's house **does not** have a garage.

_____

4 You **do not** have any sisters.

_____

5 The village **does not** have any stores.

_____

28.6 REWRITE THE STATEMENTS WITHOUT CONTRACTONS

I **haven't** got a dog.
I have not got a dog.

1 You**'ve** got a beautiful necklace.

_____

2 She **hasn't** got any sisters.

_____

3 We **haven't** got a microwave.

_____

4 Greg **hasn't** got a bike.

_____

5 My **town's** got two theaters.

_____

6 Chloe **hasn't** got a cat.

_____

7 They**'ve** got a new house.

_____

28.7 LISTEN TO THE AUDIO AND MATCH THE OBJECTS WITH THEIR OWNERS

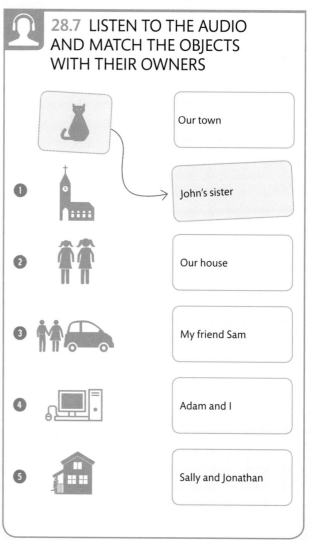

Our town

John's sister

Our house

My friend Sam

Adam and I

Sally and Jonathan

28.8 USE THE CHART TO CREATE 11 CORRECT SENTENCES AND SAY THEM OUT LOUD

I have a computer.

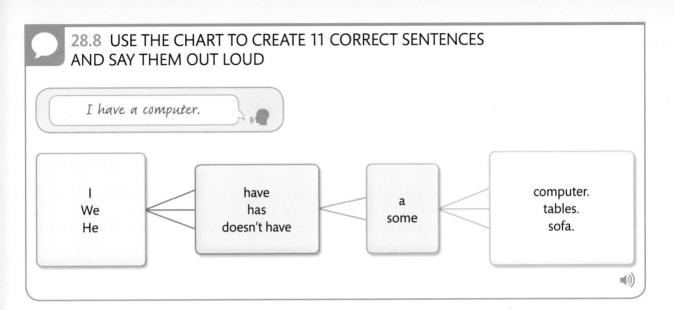

28.9 FILL IN THE GAPS TO WRITE EACH SENTENCE THREE DIFFERENT WAYS

I have a car.	I have got a car.	I've got a car.
1	She has got two bedrooms.	
2 They don't have a dog.		
3		We've got some chairs.
4	He has got a brother.	
5 Carla doesn't have a sister.		
6	You have got a car.	
7		Phil's got a dog.
8 You have a yard.		
9		Jamal hasn't got a sofa.
10	They have got a shower.	
11		May's got a couch.
12 He doesn't have a cat.		

91

29 What do you have?

Use questions with "have" to ask someone about the things they own. "Do" or "does" helps to form the question.

⚙ **New language** "Have" questions
Aa Vocabulary House and furniture
🧩 **New skill** Asking about household objects

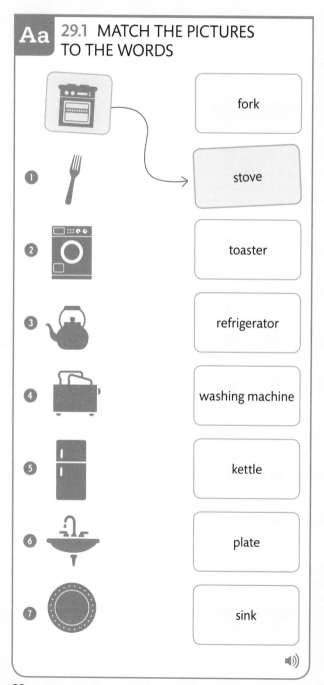

Aa 29.1 MATCH THE PICTURES TO THE WORDS

fork

1. stove

2. toaster

3. refrigerator

4. washing machine

5. kettle

6. plate

7. sink

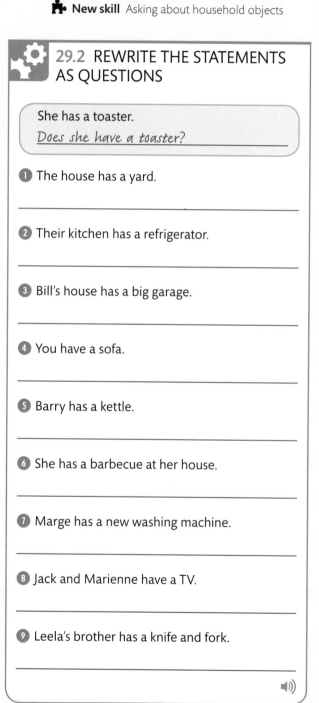

⚙ 29.2 REWRITE THE STATEMENTS AS QUESTIONS

She has a toaster.
Does she have a toaster?

1. The house has a yard.

2. Their kitchen has a refrigerator.

3. Bill's house has a big garage.

4. You have a sofa.

5. Barry has a kettle.

6. She has a barbecue at her house.

7. Marge has a new washing machine.

8. Jack and Marienne have a TV.

9. Leela's brother has a knife and fork.

29.3 LISTEN AND MATCH THE PEOPLE TO THEIR POSSESSIONS

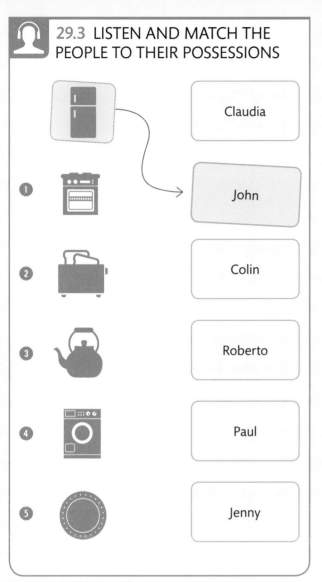

Claudia

John

Colin

Roberto

Paul

Jenny

29.4 LOOK AT THE PICTURE AND WRITE SHORT FORM ANSWERS TO EACH QUESTION

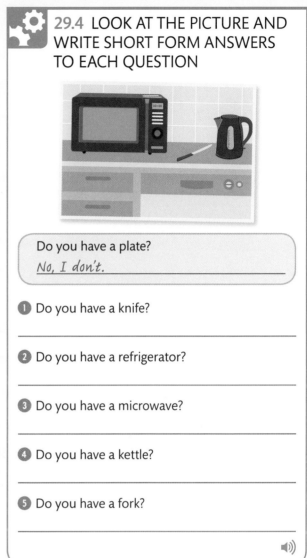

Do you have a plate?
No, I don't.

1 Do you have a knife?
_____

2 Do you have a refrigerator?
_____

3 Do you have a microwave?
_____

4 Do you have a kettle?
_____

5 Do you have a fork?
_____

29.5 USE THE CHART TO CREATE NINE CORRECT SENTENCES AND SAY THEM OUT LOUD

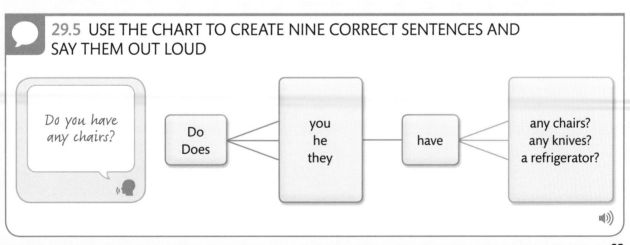

Do you have any chairs?

| Do / Does | you / he / they | have | any chairs? / any knives? / a refrigerator? |

29.6 RESPOND OUT LOUD TO THE AUDIO, FILLING IN THE GAPS

Does Kate have a necklace?

No, _____ *she doesn't* _____ .

1 Does Paula have a sofa?

Yes, _____ .

2 Does James have a snake?

Yes, _____ .

3 Does Keith have an umbrella?

No, _____ .

4 Does your town have a library?

Yes, _____ .

5 Do your parents have a car?

No, _____ .

6 Does your mom have a microwave?

No, _____ .

7 Does Gerald have a bottle?

Yes, _____ .

29.7 WRITE A QUESTION TO MATCH EACH SENTENCE

She has got a car.
Has she got a car?

1 They have got a microwave.
_____

2 Shaun and Shania have got a pet snake.
_____

3 Charles has got a camera.
_____

4 Clarissa has got a new laptop.
_____

5 Carol's house has got a big yard.
_____

6 Your friends have got my book.
_____

7 Brian has got a new TV.
_____

29.8 REWRITE THE "HAVE" QUESTIONS AS "HAVE GOT" QUESTIONS

Do you have a dog?
Have you got a dog?

1 Does the kitchen have a microwave?

2 Does your house have a yard?

3 Do the Hendersons have a car?

4 Does Claire have my glasses?

5 Do your parents have a computer?

6 Does Paul have my book?

7 Does Brian have a magazine?

8 Do your neighbors have a basement?

9 Does your cell phone have a camera?

10 Does Sam have any money?

11 Does your town have a supermarket?

12 Does Brian have a sister?

13 Do your children have a cat?

14 Does your husband have a camera?

15 Does your school have a library?

16 Does Jane have a cell phone?

17 Do the kids have their bikes?

29.9 USE THE CHART TO CREATE SEVEN CORRECT SENTENCES AND SAY THEM OUT LOUD

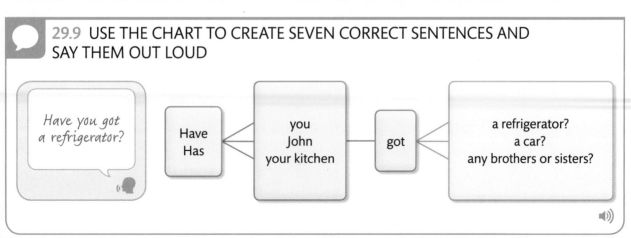

Have you got a refrigerator?

| Have / Has | you / John / your kitchen | got | a refrigerator? / a car? / any brothers or sisters? |

30 Vocabulary

Aa 30.1 FOOD AND DRINK WRITE THE WORDS FROM THE PANEL UNDER THE CORRECT PICTURES

food

1 _____

2 _____

3 _____

4 _____

8 _____

9 _____

10 _____

11 _____

12 _____

16 _____

17 _____

18 _____

19 _____

20 _____

24 _____

25 _____

26 _____

27 _____

28 _____

5 _____

6 _____

7 _____

13 _____

14 _____

15 _____

21 _____

22 _____

23 _____

29 _____

30 _____

31 _____

meat   breakfast

sugar   potatoes

bread   fruit   cheese

vegetables   drinks

strawberry   juice

apple   seafood

butter   chocolate

spaghetti   orange

water   coffee

pasta   milk

lunch   burger

eggs   ~~food~~

rice   fish   dinner

salad   cereal

banana   cake

🔊

97

31 Counting

In English, nouns can be countable or uncountable. Countable nouns can be individually counted. Objects that can't be separated and counted are uncountable.

⚙ **New language** Uncountable nouns
Aa Vocabulary Food containers
🧩 **New skill** Talking about food

⚙ **31.1 WRITE THE WORDS FROM THE PANEL IN THE CORRECT GROUPS**

COUNTABLE	UNCOUNTABLE
sandwich	water

coffee   ~~water~~   burger

rice   egg   juice

apple   ~~sandwich~~

🔊

⚙ **31.2 CROSS OUT THE INCORRECT WORD IN EACH SENTENCE**

Bob has ~~a~~ / some sugar.

① There is / are some orange juice.

② Sam has some / three milk.

③ We have a / some salt.

④ There is / are some apples.

⑤ Rita has a / some banana.

⑥ I've got a / some eggs.

🔊

⚙ **31.3 WRITE OUT WHAT EACH IMAGE SHOWS**

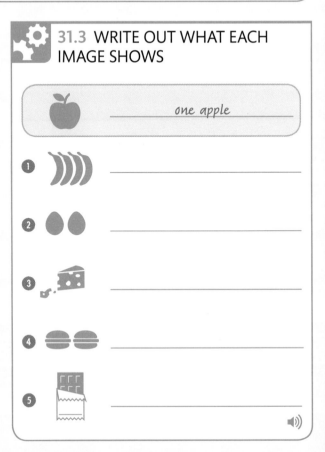

one apple

①

②

③

④

⑤

🔊

31.4 FILL IN THE GAPS TO WRITE EACH SENTENCE IN THREE DIFFERENT WAYS

Are there any apples?	There are some apples.	There aren't any apples.
① Is there any salt?		
②	There is some wine.	
③ Are there any burgers?		
④	There are some cookies.	
⑤		There aren't any pastries.
⑥ Is there any bread?		
⑦	There is some rice.	
⑧		There isn't any butter.
⑨ Are there any pizzas?		
⑩	There is some cheese.	

31.5 LISTEN TO THE AUDIO AND ANSWER THE QUESTIONS

Steve and Kate have three bags of flour.
True ☑ False ☐

① They have three bags of sugar in their cupboard.
True ☐ False ☐

② Steve and Kate haven't got any tomatoes.
True ☐ False ☐

③ They have two blocks of cheese.
True ☐ False ☐

④ Steve and Kate have got two oranges.
True ☐ False ☐

⑤ They haven't got any apples.
True ☐ False ☐

⑥ Steve and Kate don't have any coffee.
True ☐ False ☐

⑦ Kate doesn't have any chocolate.
True ☐ False ☐

⑧ Steve and Kate don't have any onions.
True ☐ False ☐

⑨ They have some rice.
True ☐ False ☐

31.6 FILL IN THE GAPS USING THE WORDS IN THE PANEL

There is a _____jar_____ of coffee.

1 There's a _____ of milk.

2 There are two _____ of rice.

3 There's a _____ of chocolate.

4 There's a _____ of juice.

5 There are three _____ of water.

6 There's a _____ of pasta.

7 There are two _____ of tea.

glass	carton	~~jar~~	bowl
cups	bar	bags	bottles

31.7 CROSS OUT THE INCORRECT WORDS IN EACH SENTENCE

There ~~is~~ / are three cartons of milk.

1 There is / are a jar of coffee.

2 There isn't / aren't any rice.

3 There is / are two cartons of juice.

4 There is / are some meat.

5 There is / are two bottles of wine.

6 There isn't / aren't any bread.

7 There is / are a bag of flour.

8 There is / are some pasta.

9 There is / are two bars of chocolate.

10 There isn't / aren't any sugar.

11 There is / are some butter.

Aa 31.8 FIND NINE WORDS FOR CONTAINERS IN THE GRID

```
K  P  D  B  O  W  L  Y  M  T
W  O  K  O  N  S  S  J  N  E
A  C  Y  T  P  S  B  O  E  E
J  Y  M  T  A  L  T  G  J  H
V  A  K  L  U  R  A  S  G  E
G  A  G  E  A  B  Z  I  B  S
R  Y  D  C  D  E  E  H  N  Q
N  W  F  G  L  D  B  Z  E  E
A  T  L  P  X  I  M  T  O  E
E  A  L  R  Y  T  K  C  S  S
R  S  C  I  D  Q  S  J  A  R
A  Q  U  Y  E  Z  D  W  T  E
N  H  P  X  O  E  C  N  N  C
K  B  T  I  B  A  R  K  D  J
Y  R  W  N  G  R  M  S  L  O
```

31.9 FILL IN THE GAPS USING "MANY" OR "MUCH"

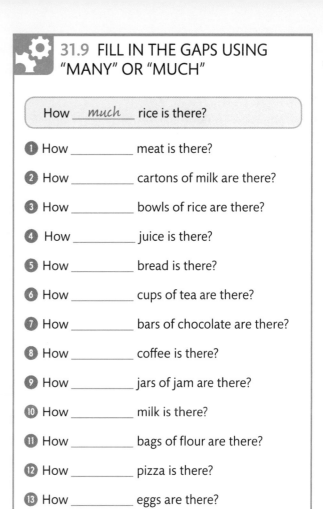

How ___much___ rice is there?

1 How _____ meat is there?

2 How _____ cartons of milk are there?

3 How _____ bowls of rice are there?

4 How _____ juice is there?

5 How _____ bread is there?

6 How _____ cups of tea are there?

7 How _____ bars of chocolate are there?

8 How _____ coffee is there?

9 How _____ jars of jam are there?

10 How _____ milk is there?

11 How _____ bags of flour are there?

12 How _____ pizza is there?

13 How _____ eggs are there?

31.10 USE THE CHART TO CREATE SIX CORRECT SENTENCES AND SAY THEM OUT LOUD

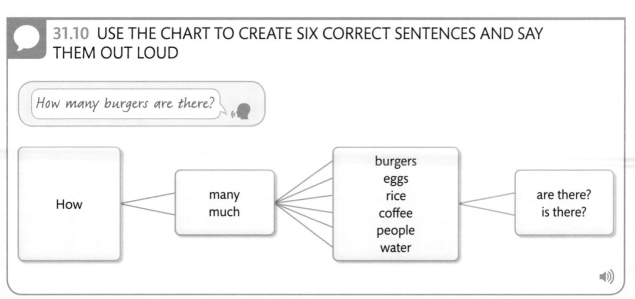

How many burgers are there?

| How | many / much | burgers / eggs / rice / coffee / people / water | are there? / is there? |

32 Measuring

Use "enough" when you have the correct number or amount of something. Use "too many" or "too much" if you have more than enough.

 New language Measurements
Aa Vocabulary Ingredients and quantities
New skill Talking about amounts

32.1 CROSS OUT THE INCORRECT WORDS IN EACH SENTENCE

We have too many / ~~too much~~ eggs.

1 There are too many / too much pears.

2 There is too many / too much milk.

3 She has too many / too much pasta.

4 We have too many / too much bananas.

5 There is too many / too much butter.

6 There are too many / too much apples.

7 There are too many / too much tomatoes.

8 I have too many / too much juice.

9 There are too many / too much mushrooms.

10 They have too many / too much burgers.

11 Sue owns too many / too much shoes.

32.2 FILL IN THE GAPS WITH "IS ENOUGH" OR "ARE ENOUGH"

There ____is enough____ flour.

1 There _____ pineapples.

2 There _____ mangoes.

3 There _____ sugar.

4 There _____ bread.

5 There _____ milk.

6 There _____ pasta.

7 There _____ apples.

8 There _____ oranges.

9 There _____ bananas.

10 There _____ chocolate.

11 There _____ eggs.

12 There _____ cheese.

13 There _____ tomatoes.

14 There _____ butter.

15 There _____ juice.

32.3 FILL IN THE GAPS TO WRITE EACH SENTENCE THREE DIFFERENT WAYS

We don't have enough salt.	We have enough salt.	We have too much salt.
1 You don't have enough oranges.		
2	There's enough sugar.	
3		We have too much butter.
4	There are enough eggs.	
5 There isn't enough flour.		
6		There are too many potatoes.
7	You have enough melons.	
8 He doesn't have enough bread.		
9		There is too much tea.
10	We have enough milk.	
11 You don't have enough rice.		
12		There are too many mangoes.
13	Martha has enough onions.	
14 You don't have enough carrots.		

32.4 LISTEN TO THE AUDIO AND ANSWER THE QUESTIONS

Bruce and Shelley don't have any bread.
True ☐ **False** ☑

1 They don't have enough butter.
True ☐ **False** ☐

2 They have too many bags of flour.
True ☐ **False** ☐

3 They don't have enough salt.
True ☐ **False** ☐

4 They have enough tomatoes.
True ☐ **False** ☐

5 They don't have enough cheese.
True ☐ **False** ☐

103

32.5 FILL IN THE GAPS USING "ENOUGH," "NOT ENOUGH," "TOO MANY," OR "TOO MUCH"

Vegetable pasta soup

1 onion
3 carrots
2 potatoes
4 tomatoes

15 oz pasta
3 fl oz oil
1 loaf of bread

Fruit cake

6 oz butter
9 oz flour
6 oz sugar
2 oranges

2 bananas
3 eggs
1 glass of milk

There are _____ *too many* _____ onions.

❶ There are _____ carrots.

❷ There are _____ potatoes.

❸ There are _____ tomatoes.

❹ There is _____ pasta.

❺ There is _____ oil.

❻ There is _____ bread.

❼ There is _____ butter.

❽ There is _____ flour.

❾ There is _____ sugar.

❿ There are _____ oranges.

⓫ There are _____ bananas.

⓬ There are _____ eggs.

⓭ There is _____ milk.

32.6 REWRITE THE SENTENCES, CORRECTING THE ERRORS

There are enough corn to make the soup.
There is enough corn to make the soup.

1. There aren't enough butter.

2. There isn't enough tomatoes.

3. There isn't enough mangoes.

4. You have too money bananas.

5. They don't have enoug butter.

6. There is enough onions.

7. There aren't enough sugar.

8. You have to many pineapples.

9. They have too moch bread.

10. You dont have enough apples.

11. They have enogh flour.

12. There is too many potatoes.

13. There are too much salt.

14. There are too much chocolate.

15. There is too many mangoes.

16. You have enugh eggs.

17. There is enough oranges.

🔊

32.7 USE THE CHART TO CREATE NINE CORRECT SENTENCES AND SAY THEM OUT LOUD

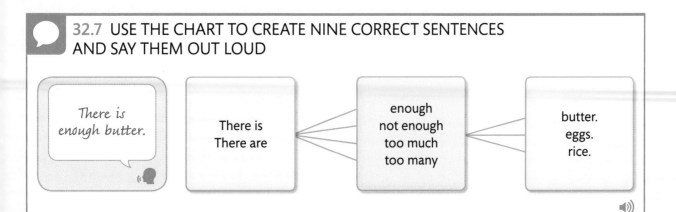

🔊

105

Aa 33.1 CLOTHES, ACCESSORIES, AND COLORS WRITE THE WORDS FROM THE PANEL UNDER THE CORRECT PICTURES

blouse

1 _____

2 _____

3 _____

4 _____

7 _____

8 _____

9 _____

10 _____

11 _____

14 _____

15 _____

16 _____

17 _____

18 _____

21 _____

22 _____

23 _____

24 _____

25 _____

5 _____

6 _____

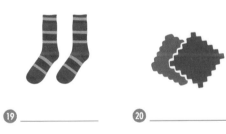

12 _____

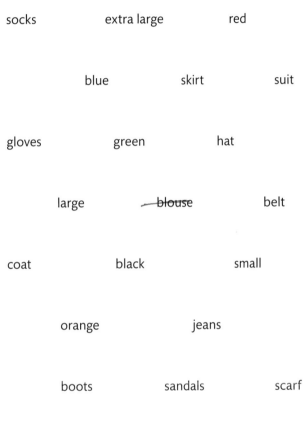

socks   extra large   red

        blue   skirt   suit

gloves   green   hat

        large   ~~blouse~~   belt

coat   black   small

        orange   jeans

        boots   sandals   scarf

shirt   medium   yellow

purple   dress   shoes

        extra small   pink

13 _____

19 _____

20 _____

26 _____

27 _____

34 At the shops

You can use many different verbs to talk about what happens when you are shopping. Use "too" and "enough" to describe how well clothes fit you.

⚙ New language Using "too" and "fit"
Aa Vocabulary Shopping and clothes
🧩 New skill Describing clothes

34.1 FILL IN THE GAPS USING THE WORDS IN THE PANEL

Jane _____owns_____ a red motorcycle.

1 That sweater _____ you. It's the right size.

2 My mom always _____ my dad's clothes.

3 These jeans don't _____. They're too small.

4 I _____ 30 pairs of shoes.

5 I always _____ clothes before I buy them.

6 Those shops _____ very fashionable clothes.

7 We _____ fruit at the market.

8 I _____ some shoes for my birthday.

9 I sometimes _____ by credit card.

chooses   fits   ~~owns~~   sell   pay   want   buy   fit   try on   own

🔊

34.2 REWRITE THE SENTENCES, CORRECTING THE ERRORS

Sally always choose her husband's clothes.
Sally always chooses her husband's clothes.

1 Ruth do a lot of her shopping on the internet.

2 The shop don't sell my size of clothes.

3 She wear short skirts.

4 Greg's jeans doesn't fit him.

5 Amy own a lot of fashionable clothes.

6 We pays for our shopping with cash.

7 Duncan never try on clothes before he buys them.

8 My parents usually pays for my clothes.

9 Peter don't own many clothes.

🔊

34.3 REWRITE THE SENTENCES, CORRECTING THE ERRORS

> Kim **want** a blue skirt.
> *Kim wants a blue skirt.*

1 That blouse **don't** fit you.

_____

2 Sue always **try** on her new clothes.

_____

3 Rob **want** a new tie for Christmas.

_____

4 Peter **buy** his meat at the butcher's shop.

_____

5 Jose **own** a beautiful house in France.

_____

6 My jeans **doesn't** fit me. They're too big.

_____

7 Samantha **choose** high-quality clothes.

_____

8 They **sells** vegetables in the market.

_____

9 Do you **wants** a new shirt for your birthday?

_____

🔊

Aa **34.4 CROSS OUT THE INCORRECT ADJECTIVE IN EACH SENTENCE**

 This is a **long** / ~~short~~ dress.

1 This is a **new** / **old** T-shirt.

2 These are **short** / **long** jeans.

3 This is an **cheap** / **expensive** tie.

4 This is a **large** / **small** sweater.

5 This is a **pink** / **blue** dress.

6 This is an **new** / **old** T-shirt.

7 These are **old** / **cheap** shoes.

8 This is a **long** / **short** skirt.

9 This is a **red** / **blue** shirt.

10 These are **big** / **small** shoes.

11 This is a **large** / **small** sweater.

 🔊

34.5 LISTEN TO THE AUDIO AND ANSWER THE QUESTIONS

 Jane and Ruth are describing the clothes they want to buy.

What type of cardigan does Jane buy?

red and short ☐

blue and long ☐

black and long ☑

① What does Jane want to buy?

a red shirt ☐

a red skirt ☐

a blue skirt ☐

② What does Ruth want to buy for her mother?

a red scarf ☐

yellow gloves ☐

a red hat ☐

❸ What does Ruth want to buy?

brown shoes ☐

black shoes ☐

brown boots ☐

❹ What does Jane want next?

blue jeans ☐

black jeans ☐

purple jeans ☐

❺ Jane then tries on the...

black coat. ☐

red coat. ☐

green coat. ☐

Aa 34.6 FIND FIVE ADJECTIVES IN THE GRID

```
D F S P F Q A T E H
C E S T L S S T F Y
H S S C O H Y C Z N
E X L G N S I M E L
A T E P G H X U R H
P I W S R O G X E E
B P A H A R D R P I
N C S O F T E I H R
```

Aa 34.7 MATCH THE PHRASES THAT MEAN THE SAME

not big enough → too small

too expensive

① not soft enough

too short

② not new enough → too small

③ not cheap enough

too soft

④ not short enough

too hard

⑤ not hard enough

too long

⑥ not long enough

too old

🔊

110

34.8 SAY THE SENTENCES OUT LOUD, FILLING IN THE GAPS USING THE PHRASES IN THE PANEL

Sharon's dress is _too long_ .

❶ Claire's hat is
_____ .

❷ These shoes are
_____ .

❸ Sophie's pullover is
_____ .

❹ Corrine's coat is
_____ .

❺ Emma's sweater is
_____ .

❻ Chloe's scarf is
_____ .

❼ Phoebe's shoes are
_____ .

❽ Joshua's jacket is
_____ .

| too big | ~~too long~~ | too small | big enough | too long |
| too small | too big | too expensive | too small | |

35 Describing things

You can use adjectives to give your opinion
about things as well as to give factual information.
You can use more than one adjective before a noun.

⚙ **New language** Opinion adjectives
Aa Vocabulary Shopping and materials
🧩 **New skill** Giving opinions

📖 **35.1 READ THE BLOG AND ANSWER THE QUESTIONS**

Fashion Blog

HOME | ENTRIES | ABOUT | CONTACT

POSTED SATURDAY, MAY 3
My next shopping trip...

Well, it's only spring, but I've got big plans about what I want to buy for the summer! I
have some lovely red cotton trousers, but I want to buy some pink ones, too. I have this
horrible green sweatshirt, which was a present from my friend. So I really want to buy a
new sweatshirt. I want a red one!

I want some new shoes. I have some pretty yellow sandals and some sneakers, but I
want to buy some heels. Leather is very trendy this year. I have a gorgeous brown
leather jacket from Spain. But I want to buy some leather boots. I have lots of woolen
hats for the winter. But I really want to buy a nice yellow one. I want to go to Malta in the
summer, so I want to look good. Happy shopping everyone!

Jane has some red cotton trousers.
True ✓ **False** ☐

① Jane has a horrible blue sweatshirt.
True ☐ **False** ☐

② She wants a red sweatshirt.
True ☐ **False** ☐

③ She has some yellow sandals.
True ☐ **False** ☐

④ Jane wants some heels.
True ☐ **False** ☐

⑤ She has a brown leather jacket from Greece.
True ☐ **False** ☐

⑥ She wants some leather boots.
True ☐ **False** ☐

⑦ She doesn't have many winter hats.
True ☐ **False** ☐

⑧ She wants to buy a yellow hat.
True ☐ **False** ☐

⑨ Jane wants to go to Italy this summer.
True ☐ **False** ☐

35.2 MARK THE SENTENCES THAT ARE CORRECT

This is a beautiful green blouse. ☑
This is a green beautiful blouse. ☐

1 Our house has a pretty little yard. ☐
Our house has a little pretty yard. ☐

2 James has a leather ugly jacket. ☐
James has an ugly leather jacket. ☐

3 Pete has a wooden old table. ☐
Pete has an old wooden table. ☐

4 This is a brilliant new book. ☐
This is a new brilliant book. ☐

5 Shelley's got a beautiful glass bottle. ☐
Shelley's got a glass beautiful bottle. ☐

6 That was such a boring old film. ☐
That was such an old boring film. ☐

7 That's an ugly woolen sweater. ☐
That's a woolen ugly sweater. ☐

8 Those are black boring shoes. ☐
Those are boring black shoes. ☐

9 I've got a horrible old car. ☐
I've got an old horrible car. ☐

10 Simone has a beautiful gray parrot. ☐
Simone has a gray beautiful parrot. ☐

11 That's an old horrible house! ☐
That's a horrible old house! ☐

12 You've got a red nice shirt. ☐
You've got a nice red shirt. ☐

🔊

Aa 35.3 REWRITE THE SENTENCES, PUTTING THE WORDS IN THE CORRECT ORDER

| a | It's | green | hat. | lovely |

It's a lovely green hat.

1 | beautiful | Jill's | got | dog. | a | black |

_____

2 | new | nice | has | house. | a | Simon |

_____

3 | ugly | have | old | an | car. | They |

_____

4 | red | pretty | are | shoes. | Those |

_____

5 | pink | an | ugly | hat. | That's |

_____

6 | a | has | brown | horrible | snake. | Greg |

_____

7 | got | You've | black | a | bag. | beautiful |

_____

8 | new | is | great | a | book. | This |

_____

🔊

Aa 35.4 FIND SEVEN WORDS THAT DESCRIBE WHAT THINGS ARE MADE OF

```
S H C G A I R C C A L C W
Q M E T A L K V O Q E V O
A E D E M J S D T K A D O
P L A S T I C G T T I D
B T B C X W D L O X H B N
E E P A P E R A N A E D R
R M Z W O O L S R O R Z O
K S X A E B R S L S X U X
```

35.5 LISTEN TO THE AUDIO AND ANSWER THE QUESTIONS

The shoes are...
cotton ☐ **leather** ☑ **plastic** ☐

1 The cups are...
metal ☐ **glass** ☐ **plastic** ☐

2 The table is...
wooden ☐ **plastic** ☐ **metal** ☐

3 The bottle is...
plastic ☐ **glass** ☐ **metal** ☐

4 The jacket is...
wool ☐ **leather** ☐ **plastic** ☐

5 The chairs are...
plastic ☐ **wooden** ☐ **metal** ☐

6 The sweater is...
wool ☐ **leather** ☐ **nylon** ☐

7 The table is...
metal ☐ **glass** ☐ **wooden** ☐

8 The bag is...
leather ☐ **plastic** ☐ **paper** ☐

9 The scarf is...
wool ☐ **leather** ☐ **silk** ☐

10 The bottle is...
glass ☐ **plastic** ☐ **metal** ☐

11 The bag is...
paper ☐ **plastic** ☐ **leather** ☐

12 The lamp is...
metal ☐ **glass** ☐ **wooden** ☐

13 The chairs are...
wooden ☐ **metal** ☐ **plastic** ☐

35.6 FILL IN THE GAPS USING THE WORDS IN THE PANEL

A broken _____ *glass* _____ bottle.

4 Three _____ chairs.

1 Four _____ cups.

5 A green _____ sweater.

2 An ugly _____ table.

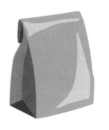

6 A brown _____ bag.

3 An old _____ jacket.

7 Beautiful _____.

| plastic | wooden | ~~glass~~ | paper | wool | leather | metal | fabric |

🔊

Aa 36.1 **SPORTS** WRITE THE WORDS FROM THE PANEL UNDER THE CORRECT PICTURES

volleyball

1 _____

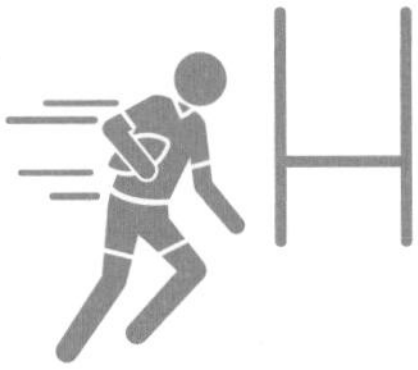

2 _____

3 _____

4 _____

5 _____

6 _____

7 _____

8 _____

9 _____

10 _____

11 _____

12 _____

13 _____

14 _____

15 _____

skateboarding   ice hockey   baseball   roller-skating   tennis

cycling   rugby   snowboarding   running   skiing   ~~volleyball~~

basketball   swimming   badminton   golf   horse riding

Aa 36.2 **EQUIPMENT AND VENUES** WRITE THE WORDS FROM THE PANEL UNDER THE CORRECT PICTURES

tennis racket

1 _____

2 _____

3 _____

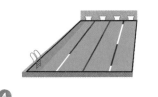

4 _____

5 _____

6 _____

7 _____

8 _____

9 _____

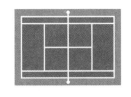

10 _____

11 _____

surfboard	baseball bat	stadium	snowboard
swimming pool	~~tennis racket~~	tennis court	skateboard
golf club	running track	skis	golf course

🔊

37 Talking about sports

To describe taking part in some sports, you use the verb "go" plus the gerund. For other sports, you use "play" plus the noun.

 New language "Go" and "play"

Aa Vocabulary Sports

New skill Talking about sports

37.1 FILL IN THE GAPS TO COMPLETE THE SENTENCES

My friend Kim ___*goes running*___ (run) three times a week in the park.

1. Douglas _____ (cycle) with his brother on Sundays.

2. Phil and John _____ (skate) in the winter.

3. Mr. Henderson _____ (sail) in the Mediterranean in the summer.

4. Veronica _____ (dance) with her friends on the weekend.

5. They _____ (hike) in the mountains in Scotland.

6. Lawrence _____ (swim) on Tuesdays.

7. Ted _____ (skateboard) on Saturday morning.

8. I _____ (ride) in France each year.

9. She _____ (shop) in Milan at Christmas.

10. We _____ (fish) after work on Mondays.

11. Anne _____ (surf) in California.

37.2 CROSS OUT THE INCORRECT SPELLINGS

We go ~~skateing~~ / skating in the park.

1 Jane goes **dancing** / danceing on Friday nights.

2 Our dad goes **sailing** / saileing in the summer.

3 I go fisheing / **fishing** in the evening.

4 Do you go **running** / runing in the morning?

5 They go **cycling** / cycleing in the summer.

6 Sam goes swiming / **swimming** on Sundays.

7 I go **horseback riding** / horseback ridding daily.

8 Claire goes **shopping** / shopeing in London.

9 Omar goes **skateboarding** / skateboardding daily.

10 Do you go **dancing** / danccing with her?

11 Rachel goes hikking / **hiking** in Peru.

12 I go **snowboarding** / snowbording in the winter.

13 Bob and Steve go surphing / **surfing** in Tahiti.

Aa 37.3 REWRITE THE VERBS AS GERUNDS

skate	=	*skating*
1 snowboard	=	_____
2 run	=	_____
3 fish	=	_____
4 swim	=	_____
5 skateboard	=	_____
6 dance	=	_____
7 surf	=	_____
8 shop	=	_____
9 cycle	=	_____
10 sail	=	_____
11 ride	=	_____

37.4 SAY THE SENTENCES OUT LOUD USING "GO" OR "GOES"

Sal __*goes*__ sailing at the lake.

1 I _____ shopping in the evening.

2 Jan _____ skateboarding on Fridays.

3 Pete _____ sailing on the weekend.

4 Sam _____ skating every December.

5 I _____ running on Wednesday.

6 They _____ fishing with their friends.

7 Sarah _____ dancing on Saturdays.

37.5 CROSS OUT THE INCORRECT WORDS

> He ~~play~~ / plays baseball on Sundays.

1. Do you play / plays chess?

2. Paolo play / plays badminton at the weekend.

3. My father play / plays golf with his friends.

4. We don't play / doesn't play baseball anymore.

5. I play / plays tennis with my brother.

6. Greg don't play / doesn't play basketball.

7. Liz play / plays racquet ball on the weekend.

8. Your dad don't play / doesn't play soccer.

9. Our dog plays / play with its ball.

10. Mike play / plays soccer on Saturdays.

11. We don't play / doesn't play golf in the winter.

12. Pammy don't play / doesn't play tennis.

◀))

37.6 REWRITE THE STATEMENTS AS QUESTIONS

> They play soccer on weekends.
> *Do they play soccer on weekends?*

1. He plays badminton on Fridays.

_____

2. Noah plays golf with his grandpa.

_____

3. They play basketball with their friends.

_____

4. Georgia plays baseball at school.

_____

5. We play tennis in the summer.

_____

6. Tim's parents play chess in the evening.

_____

◀))

37.7 LISTEN TO THE AUDIO AND ANSWER THE QUESTIONS

> Mark doesn't play golf during the week.
> **True** ☑ **False** ☐

1. Steven goes cycling in the winter.
True ☐ **False** ☐

2. Max goes running every evening.
True ☐ **False** ☐

3. Ian plays soccer four times a week.
True ☐ **False** ☐

4. Janine hates running.
True ☐ **False** ☐

5. Lila goes skating with her sister.
True ☐ **False** ☐

6. Robbie doesn't go running anymore.
True ☐ **False** ☐

7. Susan goes fishing on the weekend.
True ☐ **False** ☐

37.8 FILL IN THE GAPS WITH "GO," "GOES," "PLAY," OR "PLAYS" TO COMPLETE THE SENTENCES

They _____*go*_____ running every week.

❶ John _____ badminton on Wednesday.

❷ You _____ fishing with your brother.

❸ My uncle _____ chess with my aunt.

❹ We _____ dancing in the evening.

❺ Sally's dad _____ rugby.

❻ Bartou _____ cycling in the mountains.

❼ Ramona _____ racquet ball with her dad.

❽ Our kids _____ baseball after school.

❾ Simon and Pam _____ surfing in the summer.

❿ They _____ basketball every Saturday.

⓫ We _____ snowboarding in Austria.

37.9 LOOK AT THE PICTURES, THEN SAY THE SENTENCES OUT LOUD, FILLING IN THE GAPS

I _____*play tennis*_____ () on Mondays, Tuesdays, and Thursdays.

❶ I _____ ( ) with my friends at school.

❷ Anna _____ ( ) in the afternoon on Sundays.

❸ Mrs. Amir _____ ( ) with her husband in the evening.

❹ Max _____ ( ) on Tuesdays and Fridays.

❺ Peter _____ ( ) with his brother on Mondays and Wednesdays.

121

Aa 38.1 HOBBIES AND PASTIMES WRITE THE WORDS FROM THE PANEL UNDER THE CORRECT PICTURES

cook

1 _____

2 _____

3 _____

4 _____

7 _____

8 _____

9 _____

10 _____

11 _____

14 _____

15 _____

16 _____

17 _____

18 _____

21 _____

22 _____

23 _____

24 _____

25 _____

5 _____

6 _____

12 _____

13 _____

19 _____

20 _____

26 _____

27 _____

play cards   paint   sew

go camping   write   take photos

go out for a meal   visit a museum

~~cook~~   watch television   play chess

go shopping   read   do yoga

watch a movie   play a musical instrument

go to the gym   bake   see a play

play video games   walk / hike

meet friends   do the gardening

draw   go bird watching   knit

do puzzles   listen to music

39 Free time

Adverbs of frequency show how often you do something, from something you do very frequently ("always") to something you don't do at all ("never").

⚙ **New language** Adverbs of frequency
Aa Vocabulary Pastimes
🧩 **New skill** Talking about your free time

39.1 READ THE EMAIL AND ANSWER THE QUESTIONS

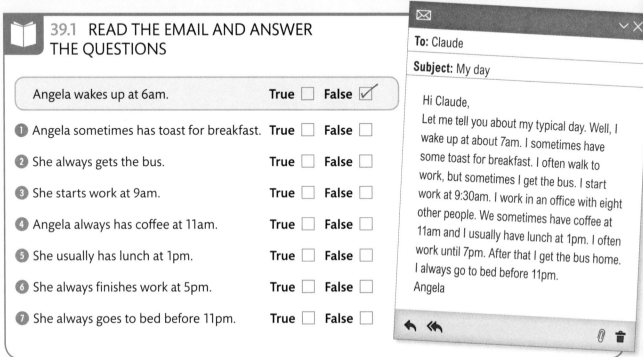

Angela wakes up at 6am. True ☐ False ☑

① Angela sometimes has toast for breakfast. True ☐ False ☐

② She always gets the bus. True ☐ False ☐

③ She starts work at 9am. True ☐ False ☐

④ Angela always has coffee at 11am. True ☐ False ☐

⑤ She usually has lunch at 1pm. True ☐ False ☐

⑥ She always finishes work at 5pm. True ☐ False ☐

⑦ She always goes to bed before 11pm. True ☐ False ☐

To: Claude

Subject: My day

Hi Claude,

Let me tell you about my typical day. Well, I wake up at about 7am. I sometimes have some toast for breakfast. I often walk to work, but sometimes I get the bus. I start work at 9:30am. I work in an office with eight other people. We sometimes have coffee at 11am and I usually have lunch at 1pm. I often work until 7pm. After that I get the bus home. I always go to bed before 11pm.

Angela

39.2 REWRITE THE SENTENCES, PUTTING THE WORDS IN THE CORRECT ORDER

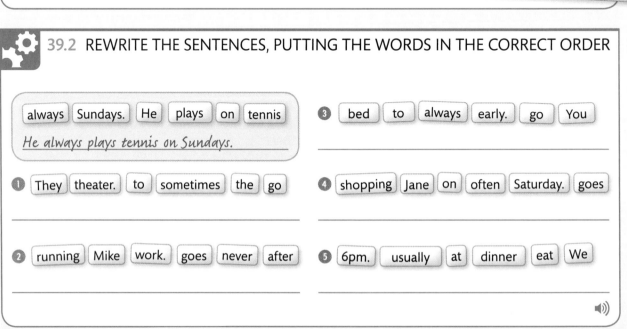

always Sundays. He plays on tennis

He always plays tennis on Sundays.

① They theater. to sometimes the go

_____

② running Mike work. goes never after

_____

③ bed to always early. go You

_____

④ shopping Jane on often Saturday. goes

_____

⑤ 6pm. usually at dinner eat We

_____

How often does John go running?

always ☐
usually ☑
sometimes ☐

① How often does Chris get up early?

never ☐
sometimes ☐
often ☐

② How often does Shelley go swimming?

never ☐
sometimes ☐
usually ☐

③ How often does Flo have tea in the morning?

sometimes ☐
often ☐
always ☐

④ How often does Sylvester go to bed at 10pm?

often ☐
usually ☐
always ☐

⑤ How often does Dominic play soccer?

never ☐
usually ☐
always ☐

⑥ How often does David read a newspaper?

sometimes ☐
often ☐
always ☐

I get up early. [rarely]

I rarely get up early.

① Clara plays chess with her grandfather. [never]

② Enzo eats chocolate ice cream. [always]

③ Paul goes fishing in the morning. [sometimes]

④ My parents drive to work. [usually]

⑤ Gill goes shopping with her mom. [never]

⑥ You go to the gym in the town. [sometimes]

⑦ Shelley watches TV in the evening. [usually]

⑧ My dog sleeps under the table. [always]

⑨ We play baseball in the summer. [sometimes]

⑩ Tim rides his horse on the weekend. [usually]

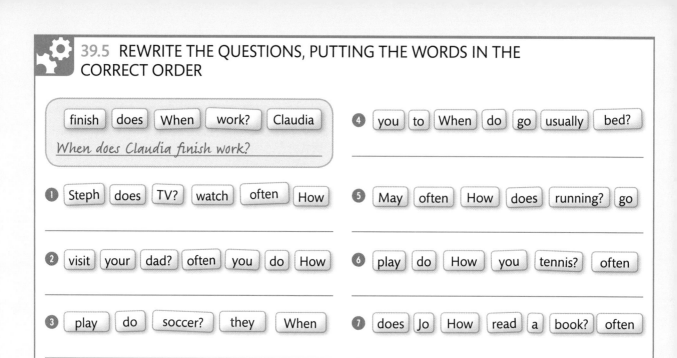

39.5 REWRITE THE QUESTIONS, PUTTING THE WORDS IN THE CORRECT ORDER

finish does When work? Claudia

When does Claudia finish work?

1. Steph does TV? watch often How

_____

2. visit your dad? often you do How

_____

3. play do soccer? they When

_____

4. you to When do go usually bed?

_____

5. May often How does running? go

_____

6. play do How you tennis? often

_____

7. does Jo How read a book? often

_____

39.6 WRITE ANSWERS TO THE QUESTIONS, FILLING IN THE GAPS

When does he go running?

_____*He goes running*_____ on Sundays.

1. When does Kelly go to the gym?

_____ on Wednesdays.

2. When does Pete play soccer?

_____ in the evening.

3. How often does Angie go to the theater?

She never _____ .

4. How often does Jake read a newspaper?

He sometimes _____ .

5. How often does she visit her family?

_____ four times a year.

6. When does Ben play baseball?

_____ every afternoon.

7. How often does Marion go shopping?

_____ twice a week.

8. When do you read a book?

_____ every evening.

9. How often does Pam make a cake?

She sometimes _____ .

39.7 REWRITE THE SENTENCES AS QUESTIONS USING "HOW OFTEN"

She goes dancing every Friday.
How often does she go dancing?

① Jimmy plays soccer once a week.

_____

② I phone my grandma twice a day.

_____

③ Sheila gets up at 7am every day.

_____

④ I read a book every evening in bed.

_____

⑤ Sally goes to work every day.

_____

⑥ I play badminton once a week.

_____

⑦ My daughter goes running every evening.

_____

⑧ Megan goes fishing twice a month.

_____

⑨ I watch TV every evening.

_____

39.8 SAY THE SENTENCES OUT LOUD, FILLING IN THE GAPS USING THE WORDS IN THE PANEL

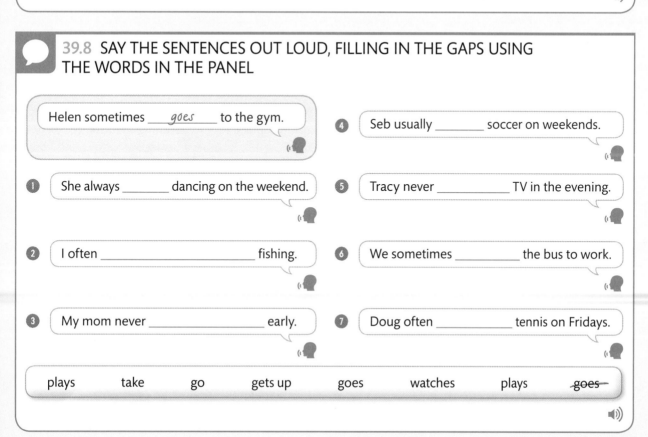

Helen sometimes ___*goes*___ to the gym.

① She always _____ dancing on the weekend.

② I often _____ fishing.

③ My mom never _____ early.

④ Seb usually _____ soccer on weekends.

⑤ Tracy never _____ TV in the evening.

⑥ We sometimes _____ the bus to work.

⑦ Doug often _____ tennis on Fridays.

| plays | take | go | gets up | goes | watches | plays | ~~goes~~ |

127

40 Likes and dislikes

Verbs such as "love," "like," and "hate" express your feelings about things. You can use these verbs with nouns or gerunds.

⚙ **New language** "Love," "like," and "hate"
Aa Vocabulary Food, sports, and pastimes
New skill Talking about what you like

Aa 40.1 MATCH THE PICTURES TO THE CORRECT SENTENCES

We love basketball.

Bill doesn't like cats.

We like cake.

I hate tennis.

Samantha likes chocolate.

I don't like pasta.

They hate board games.

Shelley loves pizza.

🎧 40.2 LISTEN TO THE AUDIO AND CHOOSE THE CORRECT ANSWERS

What does Doug like?
fruits ☐   fast food ☑

① What does Doug hate?
salad ☐   fries ☐

② What does Shelley love?
sports ☐   painting ☐

③ What does she like doing on the weekend?
playing tennis ☐   reading books ☐

④ What does she not like?
tennis ☐   golf ☐

⑤ What does Doug love doing?
watching TV ☐   listening to music ☐

⑥ What music does Doug like?
pop music ☐   classical music ☐

⑦ What does he dislike doing?
going shopping ☐   reading newspapers ☐

⑧ What does Shelley like doing in her free time?
cooking ☐   going to the cinema ☐

⑨ What does Shelley dislike?
cooking ☐   scary films ☐

⑩ What does she like doing?
taking photos ☐   visiting museums ☐

40.3 WRITE THE OPPOSITE OF EACH STATEMENT

Jack likes London.	Jack doesn't like London.
① Chris likes spiders.	
② They love Paris.	
③ Mrs. McGregor likes cats.	
④ We love soccer.	
⑤ We like wine.	
⑥ Simone loves her horse.	
⑦ He likes your necklace.	
⑧ Jean-Marie loves sports.	
⑨ Colin likes pizza.	
⑩ Douglas likes Anne.	
⑪ Cynthia hates dogs.	
⑫ We love chocolate.	
⑬ You like cheese.	
⑭ Susan likes pizza.	

🔊

40.4 USE THE CHART TO CREATE 12 CORRECT SENTENCES AND SAY THEM OUT LOUD

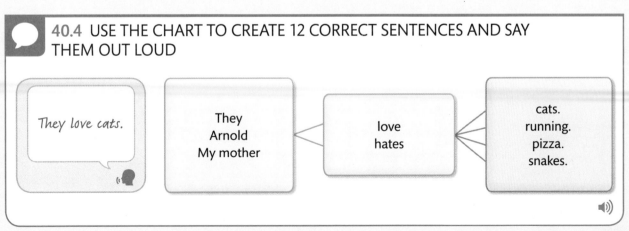

129

40.5 READ THE BLOG AND ANSWER THE QUESTIONS IN FULL SENTENCES

What is Jane's job?

She's a doctor.

① What does she like doing in her free time?

_____

② What is her favorite food?

_____

③ What does Jane not like cooking?

_____

④ What does she do on the weekend?

_____

⑤ What food does she not like?

_____

⑥ What does Jane hate?

_____

Lifestyle

HOME | ENTRIES | ABOUT | CONTACT

POSTED WEDNESDAY, MARCH 23

Jane's world

I'm Jane Petersen and I write this blog. So, what about me? Well, I'm 29 years old and come from New York. I'm a doctor, but I love cooking in my free time…

My grandmother is from Italy, so I like cooking Italian food. It's my favorite. I'm a vegetarian, so I don't like cooking meat. But I love cooking fish. On weekends I love cooking for my friends and family. What else? In my free time I like jogging, and going to the gym with my friends. What do I not like? Well, I don't like fast food. Oh, and I hate candy!

I hope you enjoy my blog!

40.6 FILL IN THE GAPS WITH THE CORRECT FORMS OF THE WORDS IN BRACKETS

Claire *does not like* (not like) swimming, but she *loves* (love) playing tennis.

① I _____ (hate) cities, but I _____ (love) the country.

② Archie _____ (like) ice cream, and he _____ (love) pizza.

③ He _____ (love) meat, but he _____ (hate) fish.

④ Francis _____ (not like) coffee, but he _____ (like) tea.

⑤ We _____ (hate) Mondays, but we _____ (love) Fridays.

⑥ My dad _____ (dislike) classical music, but he _____ (love) rock.

Aa 40.7 MATCH THE BEGINNINGS OF THE SENTENCES TO THE CORRECT ENDINGS

I hate cheese. → I think it's disgusting.

1. Sam likes watching soccer

2. Marie loves pizza.

3. I love reading history books

4. Sally doesn't like running

5. Peggy does not like eating meat

6. Paolo does not eat chocolate

7. Jemma hates snakes.

She thinks it's delicious.

because she is a vegetarian.

because it is tiring.

I think it's disgusting.

because he doesn't have a sweet tooth.

because they're really interesting.

She thinks they are scary.

because it's exciting.

40.8 READ THE EMAIL AND ANSWER THE QUESTIONS

The cafés and bars by the sea are...
boring ☐ exciting ☑ interesting. ☐

1. The weather in Sardinia is...
hot ☐ cold ☐ rainy. ☐

2. The museum in the town is really...
exciting ☐ interesting ☐ tiring. ☐

3. Si loves pizza because it is...
disgusting ☐ tiring ☐ delicious. ☐

4. Samantha hates pasta because it is...
interesting ☐ boring ☐ delicious. ☐

5. Si doesn't like walking because it's...
exciting ☐ tiring ☐ boring. ☐

To: Charles

Subject: Italy trip

Hi Charles,

We're in Sardinia on holiday. It's very hot here. There are some great cafés and bars by the ocean. They're really exciting in the evening. There's also an interesting museum in the town. I like it a lot, and there are lots of exhibits.

The food here is amazing. I love the pizza here. It's delicious. Samantha hates the pasta, though. She thinks it's really boring!

In the afternoons we go walking. Samantha loves it, but I don't! I really hate it because it's so tiring.

Hope you're all well,
Si

Aa 41.1 **MUSIC** WRITE THE WORDS FROM THE PANEL UNDER THE CORRECT PICTURES

band

1 _____

2 _____

3 _____

7 _____

8 _____

9 _____

10 _____

14 _____

15 _____

16 _____

17 _____

21 _____

22 _____

23 _____

24 _____

4 _____

5 _____

6 _____

11 _____

12 _____

13 _____

18 _____

19 _____

20 _____

25 _____

26 _____

27 _____

guitar player   orchestra

headphones   Latin

flute   sing a song

~~band~~   rap   drum

rock   saxophone   trumpet

play the trumpet   violin

dance   piano

concert   microphone

conductor   keyboard

harmonica   jazz

audience   country

album   electric guitar

opera   guitar

🔊

42 Expressing preference

You use "like" and "love" to show how much you enjoy something. "Favorite" is used to identify the thing you love most in a group.

✿ **New language** Using "favorite"
Aa Vocabulary Food and music
✚ **New skill** Talking about your favorite things

42.1 MARK THE SENTENCE THAT MATCHES EACH PICTURE

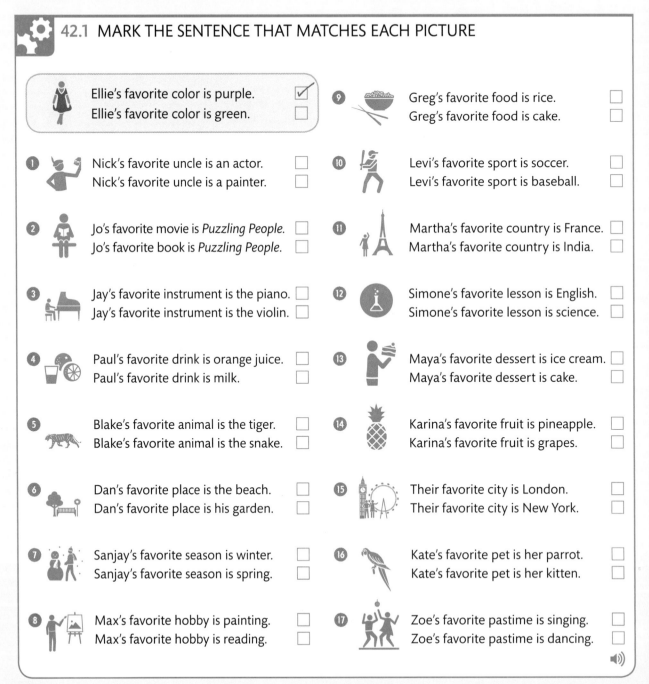

Ellie's favorite color is purple. ☑
Ellie's favorite color is green. ☐

9 Greg's favorite food is rice. ☐
Greg's favorite food is cake. ☐

1 Nick's favorite uncle is an actor. ☐
Nick's favorite uncle is a painter. ☐

10 Levi's favorite sport is soccer. ☐
Levi's favorite sport is baseball. ☐

2 Jo's favorite movie is *Puzzling People*. ☐
Jo's favorite book is *Puzzling People*. ☐

11 Martha's favorite country is France. ☐
Martha's favorite country is India. ☐

3 Jay's favorite instrument is the piano. ☐
Jay's favorite instrument is the violin. ☐

12 Simone's favorite lesson is English. ☐
Simone's favorite lesson is science. ☐

4 Paul's favorite drink is orange juice. ☐
Paul's favorite drink is milk. ☐

13 Maya's favorite dessert is ice cream. ☐
Maya's favorite dessert is cake. ☐

5 Blake's favorite animal is the tiger. ☐
Blake's favorite animal is the snake. ☐

14 Karina's favorite fruit is pineapple. ☐
Karina's favorite fruit is grapes. ☐

6 Dan's favorite place is the beach. ☐
Dan's favorite place is his garden. ☐

15 Their favorite city is London. ☐
Their favorite city is New York. ☐

7 Sanjay's favorite season is winter. ☐
Sanjay's favorite season is spring. ☐

16 Kate's favorite pet is her parrot. ☐
Kate's favorite pet is her kitten. ☐

8 Max's favorite hobby is painting. ☐
Max's favorite hobby is reading. ☐

17 Zoe's favorite pastime is singing. ☐
Zoe's favorite pastime is dancing. ☐

◀))

A group of people are talking about their favorite things.

Dave's favorite type of music in the morning is...	soul	jazz ✓	rock. ☐
❶ Jenny's favorite subject at school is...	physics ☐	math ☐	biology. ☐
❷ Mike's favorite day of the week is...	Monday ☐	Wednesday ☐	Friday. ☐
❸ Colin's favorite color is...	red ☐	yellow ☐	purple. ☐
❹ Sally's favorite dessert is...	ice cream ☐	chocolate cake ☐	apple pie. ☐
❺ Danny's favorite sport is...	soccer ☐	basketball ☐	baseball. ☐
❻ Clarice's favorite season is...	summer ☐	fall ☐	winter. ☐

⚙ **42.3 REWRITE THE SENTENCES, CORRECTING THE ERRORS**

Her love type of music is rock.
Her favorite type of music is rock.

❶ Barbara likes listen to music in the evening.

_____

❷ Arnold favorite food is ice cream and pizza.

_____

❸ Craig don't like getting up in the morning.

_____

❹ Seb's favorite type music is hip-hop.

_____

❺ Ruth like orange juice.

_____

❻ Daniel favorite animal is the lion.

_____

❼ I likes bacon and eggs for breakfast.

_____

❽ Aziz don't like lasagna or spaghetti.

_____

❾ Miguel love going to the movie theater.

_____

🔊

✉

To: Ben

Subject: My town

Hi Ben,

Netherton is small, very small. Only 800 people live here, but there's lots to do. In the morning, a lot of people take their dogs for a walk. Some people like to go to the park, but the favorite place is by the river. It's beautiful. Drinking coffee is popular here. Some people go to Dino's café, and there's a café in the supermarket. But the favorite place is Alfredo's. It's always very busy in the morning.

Dino's café is very popular at lunchtime, though, because they serve delicious pizzas there. It's the favorite place for lunch. There's a French restaurant called Chez Jean-Claude, but it's very expensive.

There's a swimming pool and a tennis court. The tennis court is the favorite place for young people to go in the summer. In the winter everyone likes to go to the swimming pool.

In the evening, there isn't much to do. There is one bar and a nightclub, but people don't like to go there. A lot of people go to the nearest city of Silchester on weekends. There are lots of nightclubs there.

Norah

📎 🗑

↩ ↩↩

Netherton is a small town.	True ✓	False ☐
❶ A lot of people walk their dogs in Netherton.	True ☐	False ☐
❷ The park is people's favorite place to walk their dogs.	True ☐	False ☐
❸ Alfredo's is always empty in the mornings.	True ☐	False ☐
❹ Dino's café is people's favorite place to drink coffee.	True ☐	False ☐
❺ Dino's is the favorite place to eat lunch.	True ☐	False ☐
❻ Chez Jean-Claude is a cheap restaurant.	True ☐	False ☐
❼ People go to the tennis court in the winter.	True ☐	False ☐
❽ The bar and disco are not very popular.	True ☐	False ☐
❾ People go to the city on weekends.	True ☐	False ☐
❿ There are lots of nightclubs in Silchester.	True ☐	False ☐

42.5 FILL IN THE GAPS USING THE WORDS IN THE PANEL

 Liz's favorite fruit is an _____ *apple* _____ .

① Arnie's favorite sport is _____ .

② Joan's favorite animal is a _____ .

③ Hassan's favorite actor is _____ .

④ Pam's favorite number is _____ .

⑤ Jane's favorite sport is _____ .

⑥ Dora's favorite ice cream is _____ .

⑦ Jim's favorite food is _____ .

spaghetti

Chris Minota

tennis

~~apple~~

strawberry

dolphin

21

badminton

🔊

💬 42.6 USE THE CHART TO CREATE 14 CORRECT SENTENCES AND SAY THEM OUT LOUD

She loves salsa dancing. 🗣🔊

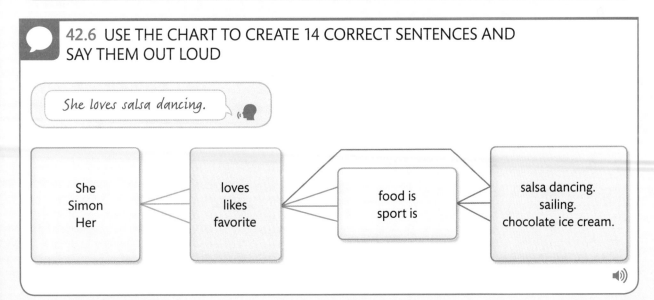

🔊

Aa 43.1 ABILITIES WRITE THE WORDS FROM THE PANEL UNDER THE CORRECT PICTURES

____whisper____

❶ _____

❷ _____

❸ _____

❼ _____

❽ _____

❾ _____

❿ _____

⑭ _____

⑮ _____

⑯ _____

⑰ _____

㉑ _____

㉒ _____

㉓ _____

㉔ _____

4 _____

5 _____

6 _____

11 _____

12 _____

13 _____

18 _____

19 _____

20 _____

25 _____

26 _____

27 _____

act   lift

drive   catch

work   jump

~~whisper~~   listen

sit   understand

subtract   fly

kick   climb

shout   spell

make (a snowman)

add   throw

move   hit

carry   see

stand up   walk

talk   ride

do (homework)

139

44 What you can and can't do

Use "can" to talk about the things you are able to do, such as ride a bicycle or play the guitar. Use "cannot" or "can't" for things you are not able to do.

⚙ **New language** "Can," "can't," and "cannot"
Aa Vocabulary Talents and abilities
🧩 **New skill** Say what you can and can't do

44.1 FILL IN THE GAPS TO WRITE EACH SENTENCE THREE DIFFERENT WAYS

I can read Russian.	I cannot read Russian.	I can't read Russian.
❶ _____	I cannot ride a horse.	_____
❷ I can climb a tree.	_____	_____
❸ _____	_____	I can't speak French.
❹ _____	I cannot sing.	_____
❺ _____	_____	I can't lift a box.
❻ _____	I cannot fly a kite.	_____
❼ I can catch a fish.	_____	_____
❽ _____	I cannot swim.	_____

44.2 REWRITE THE SENTENCES, CORRECTING THE ERRORS

Ben **can't to cook** paella.
Ben can't cook paella.

❶ Kate **can hitting** the ball.
_____

❷ Paul **can't to do** math.
_____

❸ Helen **can to spell** very well.
_____

❹ Ivan **can't running** very fast.
_____

❺ Sara **can to move** the chair.
_____

❻ Alex **can't to play** badminton.
_____

❼ Lynn **can riding** a bicycle.
_____

🔊

44.3 REWRITE THE SENTENCES, PUTTING THE WORDS IN THE CORRECT ORDER

that | chair. | can | Sylvia | carry
Sylvia can carry that chair.

1 drive | car. | Eliza | cannot | a

_____

2 piano. | Jonathan | play | can | the

_____

3 jump | very | can't | high. | Cathy

_____

4 stick. | can | a | Mick | throw

_____

5 math. | can't | Laura | do

_____

6 lift | can | the | Alan | box.

_____

7 far. | very | can't | Julia | swim

_____

44.4 LISTEN TO THE AUDIO AND MARK WHETHER INA CAN OR CAN'T DO THE ACTIVITY IN EACH PICTURE

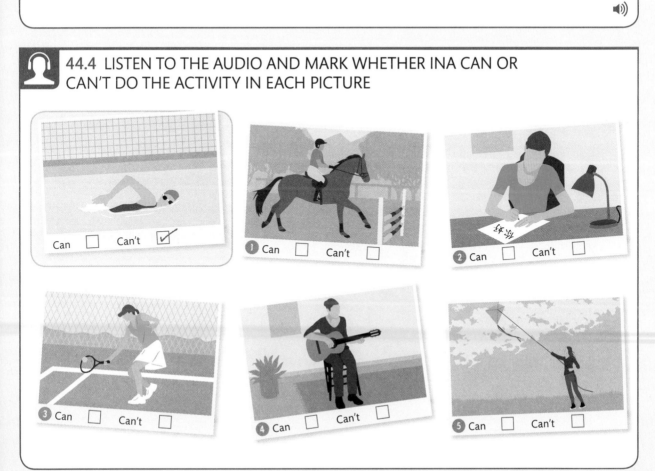

Can ☐ Can't ☑

1 Can ☐ Can't ☐

2 Can ☐ Can't ☐

3 Can ☐ Can't ☐

4 Can ☐ Can't ☐

5 Can ☐ Can't ☐

44.5 REWRITE THE STATEMENTS AS QUESTIONS

Paul and Mary can speak Russian.
Can Paul and Mary speak Russian?

⑤ Jack can climb a tree.

_____

❶ Maria and Juan can spell English words.

_____

⑥ He can't carry that box. It's too heavy.

_____

❷ The children can't do their math homework.

_____

⑦ Carlos can kick a football.

_____

❸ I can't sing difficult jazz songs.

_____

⑧ Adam and Ella can dance the tango.

_____

❹ Mark can't ride a horse.

_____

⑨ Peter and John can't swim.

_____

🔊

44.6 FILL IN THE GAPS USING THE PHRASES IN THE PANEL

Janet is a chef at a five star restaurant. She can _____ *cook very well* _____ .

❶ Jack is a diving teacher. He can _____ .

❷ Carla lives on a farm. She can _____ and look after animals.

❸ Bobby is good at languages. He can _____ .

❹ Nuna likes going on winter vacations. She can _____ .

❺ Jim is a great children's teacher. He can _____ well.

| speak Russian | ~~cook very well~~ | ski well | tell stories | swim very well | ride a horse |

🔊

44.7 RESPOND OUT LOUD TO THE AUDIO, FILLING IN THE GAPS

Can you lift a heavy box?

Yes, _I can._

1 Can you jump over the wall?

Yes, _____

2 Can you catch that big fish?

No, _____

3 Can you throw a stick for the dog?

Yes, _____

4 Can you speak Italian?

No, _____

5 Can you play the violin?

No, _____

6 Can you climb that tree?

Yes, _____

7 Can you do Sudoku puzzles?

No, _____

8 Can you sing?

No, _____

9 Can you ride a bicycle?

No, _____

10 Can you move the kitchen table?

Yes, _____

11 Can you cook roast chicken?

Yes, _____

44.8 USE THE CHART TO CREATE 18 CORRECT SENTENCES AND SAY THEM OUT LOUD

I can ride a bicycle.

| I / She / They | can / can't | ride a bicycle. / swim a mile. / play tennis. |

45 Describing actions

Words such as "quietly" and "loudly" are called adverbs. They give more information about verbs, so you can use them to describe how you do something.

⚙️ **New language** Regular and irregular adverbs
Aa **Vocabulary** Hobbies and activities
🧩 **New skill** Describing activities

45.1 FILL IN THE GAPS USING THE ADVERBS IN THE PANEL

Sanjay plays the guitar ___badly___ .

③ Alan can speak German _____ .

① My friend speaks too _____ .

④ My dog can run very _____ .

② A turtle walks very _____ .

⑤ I get up very _____ .

| early | well | quietly | slowly | fast | ~~badly~~ |

🔊

45.2 REWRITE EACH SENTENCE IN ITS OTHER FORM

| Sally speaks Japanese well. | *Sally's good at speaking Japanese.* |

① Patrick dances well. | _____

② _____ | Caitlin is good at baking.

③ My mother writes well. | _____

④ _____ | Ethan is good at playing the guitar.

⑤ Aimee skis well. | _____

⑥ _____ | They are good at swimming.

⑦ We speak English well. | _____

⑧ _____ | Lara is good at climbing trees.

45.3 REWRITE THE SENTENCES, CORRECTING THE ERRORS

> My sister dances very good.
> _My sister dances very well._

1 Haruda sometimes arrives lately for school.

_____

2 My cousin Paul runs quick.

_____

3 Shelley sings beautiful.

_____

4 Our neighbors talk so noisy at night.

_____

5 Rosa reads very slow.

_____

6 I can pass this exam easy.

_____

7 My aunt drives very careful.

_____

8 Anita works very hardly.

_____

9 We usual go to bed at 11pm.

_____

10 Angela speaks English bad.

_____

11 A cheetah runs very fastly.

_____

12 Sarah eats her food very quick.

_____

13 Andrew does his homework good.

_____

🔊

45.4 USE THE CHART TO CREATE 18 CORRECT SENTENCES AND SAY THEM OUT LOUD

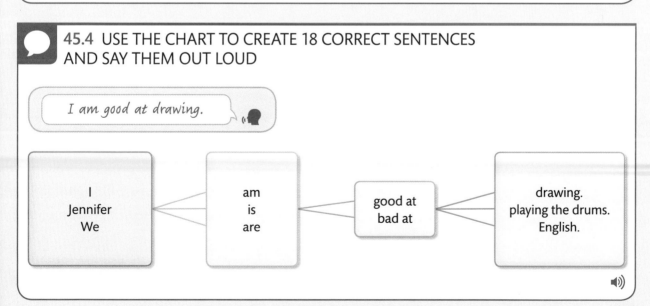

🔊

46 Describing ability

Words such as "quite" and "very" are modifying adverbs.
You can use them before other adverbs to give more
information about how you do something.

⚙ **New language** Modifying adverbs
Aa Vocabulary Skills and abilities
New skill Saying how well you do things

46.1 MARK THE SENTENCES THAT ARE CORRECT

Your cousin at skiing is very good. ☐
Your cousin is very good at skiing. ☑

① Pedro is really good at history. ☐
Pedro really good is at history. ☐

② You speak really well French. ☐
You speak French really well. ☐

③ Sandra is very good at singing. ☐
Sandra very good is at singing. ☐

④ Sal is at skiing quite good. ☐
Sal is quite good at skiing. ☐

⑤ Very well your uncle can swim. ☐
Your uncle can swim very well. ☐

⑥ They quite fast can run. ☐
They can run quite fast. ☐

⑦ Mr. Henderson is really good at golf. ☐
At golf Mr. Henderson is really good. ☐

◀))

46.2 REWRITE THE SENTENCES, PUTTING THE WORDS IN THE CORRECT ORDER

quite   soccer.   good at   is   playing   Tim

Tim is quite good at playing soccer.

① isn't   at   very   art and design.   good   Arnold

_____

② is   English.   speaking   really   cousin   good   at   My

_____

③ is   at   climbing   Jean   quite   mountains.   good

_____

◀))

146

46.3 FILL IN THE GAPS TO WRITE EACH SENTENCE USING "WELL" OR "GOOD AT"

Sam and Pauline are very good at singing. | *Sam and Pauline sing very well.*

1. _____ | My aunt speaks Polish quite well.

2. Your brother is really good at surfing. | _____

3. Katie is very good at painting. | _____

4. _____ | Silvia sings really well.

5. _____ | Martina dances very well.

6. Serge is quite good at cooking. | _____

7. _____ | Sonia plays chess really well.

8. Ricky is very good at running. | _____

9. _____ | Peter draws quite well.

10. My mom is really good at speaking Greek. | _____

11. _____ | David plays the drums very well.

46.4 SAY THE SENTENCES OUT LOUD, PUTTING THE MODIFYING ADVERBS IN THE CORRECT PLACES

My brother can run fast. [very]

My brother can run very fast.

1. Charlotte can ski well. [quite]

2. Harry sings quietly. [really]

3. My aunt walks slowly. [very]

4. Elizabeth speaks Russian well. [very]

5. My dog can jump high. [quite]

6. William speaks Japanese badly. [really]

7. Philip eats noisily. [quite]

47 Wishes and desires

You can use "I want" and "I would like" to talk about things you want to do. You can also use their negative form to say what you would not like to do.

 New language "Would" and "want"
Aa Vocabulary Leisure activities
New skill Talking about ambitions

47.1 FILL IN THE GAPS TO WRITE EACH SENTENCE THREE DIFFERENT WAYS

I want to buy a house.	I would like to buy a house.	I'd like to buy a house.
1 _____	She would like to have a cat.	_____
2 They want to visit Tokyo.	_____	_____
3 _____	_____	I'd like to eat an orange.
4 _____	You would like to learn Spanish.	_____
5 _____	_____	We'd like to go to a café.
6 He wants to live in Germany.	_____	_____
7 _____	We would like to swim in a lake.	_____

Aa 47.2 MATCH THE PICTURES TO THE CORRECT SENTENCES

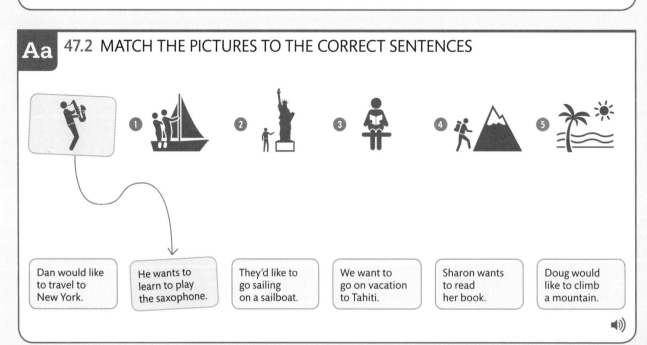

Dan would like to travel to New York.

He wants to learn to play the saxophone.

They'd like to go sailing on a sailboat.

We want to go on vacation to Tahiti.

Sharon wants to read her book.

Doug would like to climb a mountain.

148

47.3 REWRITE THE SENTENCES WITH THE MISSING WORDS IN THE CORRECT PLACES

She would like go to Paris. [to]
She would like to go to Paris.

1 Douglas to have pasta. [wants]

_____

2 They'd to go home tomorrow. [like]

_____

3 Does Chris want go swimming later? [to]

_____

4 Sheila doesn't to see Paul. [want]

_____

5 Would you to visit us tomorrow? [like]

_____

6 Our children want go to college. [to]

_____

7 She'd to buy a new cell phone. [like]

_____

8 Jenny to go shopping on Friday. [wants]

_____

9 Simon like to be a doctor. [would]

_____

10 I like to have a hamburger. [would]

_____

11 Would like to be a vet? [you]

_____

12 Chloe want to eat that pizza. [doesn't]

_____

13 You want to read this book? [Do]

_____

14 They like to watch TV. [would]

_____

15 She wants go to the party. [to]

_____

🔊

47.4 USE THE CHART TO CREATE 12 CORRECT SENTENCES AND SAY THEM OUT LOUD

I'd like to drive to Miami.

| I'd like / We want / Greg wants | to drive / to travel | to Miami. / around America. |

🔊

47.5 LISTEN TO THE AUDIO AND ANSWER THE QUESTIONS

Two friends are talking about what they want to do.

> Does Pete want to play basketball later?
> **Yes, he does.** ☐ **No, he doesn't.** ☑

1 Would Pete like to read his book?
Yes, he would. ☐ **No, he wouldn't.** ☐

2 Does Pete want to stay at home tomorrow?
Yes, he does. ☐ **No, he doesn't.** ☐

3 Would Pete like to go shopping?
Yes, he would. ☐ **No, he wouldn't.** ☐

4 Does Kat want to buy a new dress?
Yes, she does. ☐ **No, she doesn't.** ☐

5 Does Kat want to go to see a movie?
Yes, she does. ☐ **No, she doesn't.** ☐

6 Does Pete want to go to a French restaurant?
Yes, he does. ☐ **No, he doesn't.** ☐

7 Does Kat want to order spaghetti at the restaurant?
Yes, she does. ☐ **No, she doesn't.** ☐

47.6 REWRITE THE SENTENCES, PUTTING THE WORDS IN THE CORRECT ORDER

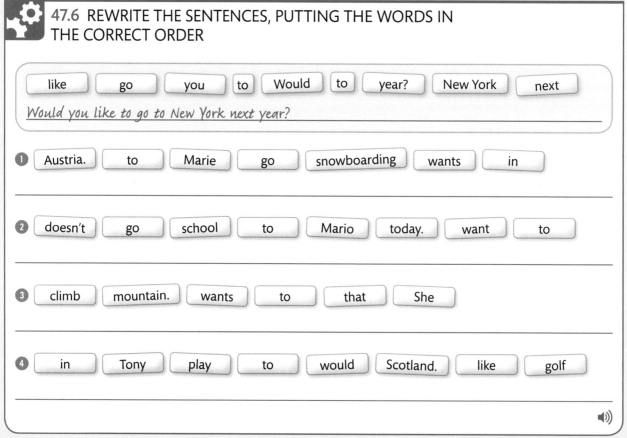

| like | go | you | to | Would | to | year? | New York | next |

Would you like to go to New York next year?

1 | Austria. | to | Marie | go | snowboarding | wants | in |

2 | doesn't | go | school | to | Mario | today. | want | to |

3 | climb | mountain. | wants | to | that | She |

4 | in | Tony | play | to | would | Scotland. | like | golf |

47.7 REWRITE THE SENTENCES, CORRECTING THE ERRORS

Would you want to go home?
Would you like to go home?

① Do you want go home now?

② Claude would likes to learn French.

③ He would likes to go swimming.

④ Paolo wants get a new cat.

⑤ Would you like visit China?

⑥ He's like to go to work later today.

⑦ Peter want to go to college next year.

⑧ They doesn't want to go to school today.

⑨ My sister want to go to Greece this summer.

47.8 SAY THE SENTENCES OUT LOUD AS QUESTIONS

She wants to play chess.
Does she want to play chess?

① Peter would like to go fishing.

② Marion wants to play tennis on Saturday.

③ He'd like to visit India.

④ Mr. Evans would like to play chess tonight.

⑤ We'd like to play squash this evening.

⑥ Sam wants to go to the park again.

⑦ They'd like to travel around China.

48 Studying

When talking about your studies you can use "I would" and "I want" to say which subjects you would like to learn. Use adverbs to say how much you want to do them.

⚙ **New language** Adverbs and articles
Aa Vocabulary Academic subjects
🧩 **New skill** Talking about your studies

48.1 REWRITE THE SENTENCES, PUTTING THE WORDS IN THE CORRECT ORDER

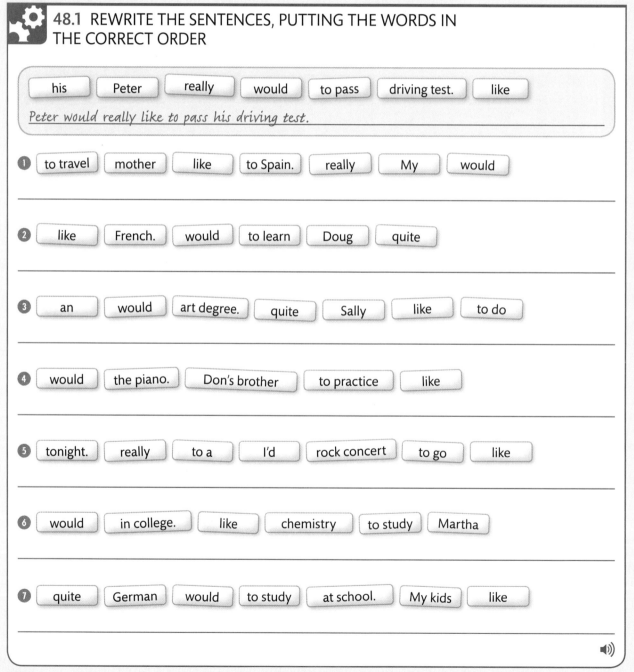

| his | Peter | really | would | to pass | driving test. | like |

Peter would really like to pass his driving test.

1. | to travel | mother | like | to Spain. | really | My | would |

2. | like | French. | would | to learn | Doug | quite |

3. | an | would | art degree. | quite | Sally | like | to do |

4. | would | the piano. | Don's brother | to practice | like |

5. | tonight. | really | to a | I'd | rock concert | to go | like |

6. | would | in college. | like | chemistry | to study | Martha |

7. | quite | German | would | to study | at school. | My kids | like |

🔊

48.2 SAY THE SENTENCES OUT LOUD, ADDING THE MODIFIER

She'd like to do a French degree. [quite]

She'd quite like to do a French degree.

① Edith would like to read her new book. [really]

② They'd like to go to a concert. [really]

③ I'd like to go to France on vacation. [really]

④ Jean-Paul would like to speak to you. [quite]

⑤ We'd like to eat pizza tonight. [quite]

⑥ Jeremy would like to play his piano. [really]

⑦ They'd like to pass their chemistry exam. [really]

⑧ Sophie would like to speak Mandarin. [quite]

⑨ David would like to visit his son. [really]

48.3 USE THE CHART TO CREATE 14 CORRECT SENTENCES AND SAY THEM OUT LOUD

I'd really like to improve my English.

| I'd / Sam would / We'd | really / quite | like | to improve my English. / to learn Japanese. / to do a history degree. |

Aa 48.4 FIND EIGHT SCHOOL TERMS IN THE PANEL IN THE GRID

```
M G D P R D R A M A
U A V R E H K Q V H
S E T A V J E D S I
I T V H I M X E E S
C S U R E V A G E T
E A D D W R M R D O
R M Z C Y H S E T R
K A K E L K X E Y Y
F N A R H M S U A N
```

review	music	study	drama
~~history~~	math	degree	exams

 48.5 CROSS OUT THE INCORRECT WORDS IN EACH SENTENCE

Jim went to bed / ~~the bed~~ hours ago.

1. Phillipa goes to college / the college.

2. Rome is beautiful city / a beautiful city.

3. We are at home / the home at the moment.

4. Sharon goes to the school / school at 9am.

5. College / The college is far away.

6. Peter goes to bed / the bed at 10pm.

7. My uncle is at mosque / the mosque today.

8. Jim goes to church / the church on Sundays.

9. Sean leaves home / a home at 7:30am.

10. Seb lives next to hospital / the hospital.

🔊

 48.6 MARK THE SENTENCES THAT ARE CORRECT

Shirley works in the hospital in Bigton. ☑
Shirley works in hospital in Bigton. ☐

1. Carol leaves work at 6pm every day. ☐
   Carol leaves a work at 6pm every day. ☐

2. Jane can drive you to school tomorrow. ☐
   Jane can drive you to a school tomorrow. ☐

3. Chris lives across from hospital. ☐
   Chris lives across from the hospital. ☐

4. Carl is at a home at the moment. ☐
   Carl is at home at the moment. ☐

5. Julia has beautiful horse. ☐
   Julia has a beautiful horse. ☐

6. The hospital isn't very far. ☐
   Hospital isn't very far. ☐

7. We go to bed at 11pm usually. ☐
   We go to the bed at 11pm usually. ☐

8. Ottersley is a beautiful town. ☐
   Ottersley is beautiful town. ☐

9. Your shoes are under bed. ☐
   Your shoes are under the bed. ☐

🔊

48.7 REWRITE THE SENTENCES, CORRECTING THE ERRORS

> Does your sister work in school?
> _Does your sister work in a school?_

1 Sally is in the hospital. She is ill.

_____

2 York is the pretty town.

_____

3 She is at a home now.

_____

4 Lizzie goes to the church on Sundays.

_____

5 Bob is at the work at the moment.

_____

6 Christopher has new car.

_____

7 Jim goes to the bed early on Sundays.

_____

8 Carlos is the very talented boy.

_____

9 Sarah and John are great team.

_____

10 Mary bought the three new pens.

_____

11 He jumped into a water and started swimming.

_____

12 New York is the beautiful city.

_____

13 A children were playing in the sun.

_____

14 I can't play the soccer on Monday.

_____

15 Can you play a classical guitar?

_____

◀))

48.8 LISTEN TO THE AUDIO AND MATCH THE PICTURES TO THE NAMES

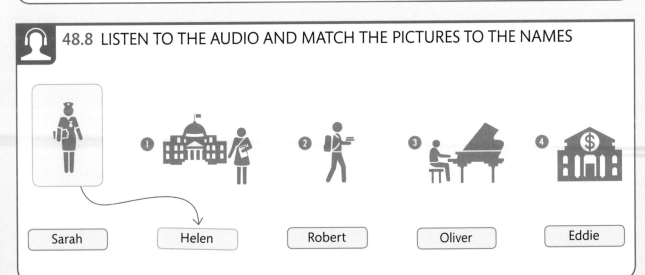

Sarah   Helen   Robert   Oliver   Eddie

Transcripts of listening exercises

UNIT 1

1.2.1 Hi! My name's Peter.

1.2.2 Hello! I'm Jo.

1.2.3 Hi! My name's Rachel.

1.2.4 Hello there! I'm Terry.

1.2.5 Hello! My name's Simone.

1.2.6 Hi! I'm Carl.

1.4 ex: R-A-C-H-E-L H-A-R-P-E-R

1.4.1 N-O-A-H A-N-D-E-R-S-O-N

1.4.2 M-A-S-O-N H-U-G-H-E-S

1.4.3 E-L-I S-A-N-D-E-R-S

1.4.4 A-L-I-C-I-A

1.4.5 Z-O-E S-P-I-E-G-E-L-M-A-N

1.4.6 B-E-N

1.4.7 N-O-R-A J-A-M-E-S

1.4.8 A-M-I-R A-N-S-A-R-I

1.4.9 N-I-N-A E-D-W-A-R-D-S

1.4.10 L-U-C-Y

1.4.11 A-M-A-N S-H-A-R-M-A

1.4.12 A-I-D-E-N

1.4.13 K-E-I-T-H

1.4.14 F-I-O-N-A

1.4.15 J-A-M-E-S T-H-O-M-A-S

UNIT 6

6.2

Rachel: Hi, Mom. Let me show you some of my boyfriend Sam's family.

Mom: Oh! That sounds interesting, Rachel!

Rachel: Well, this is Angela. She's Sam's grandmother. She's 80. And next to her is Arthur, Sam's grandfather. He's French.

Mom: And this man?

Rachel: That's Frank, Sam's father.

Mom: Oooh! He looks nice.

Rachel: Here's Charlotte. She's Sam's mother.

Mom: She's very tall, isn't she?

Rachel: And this is Micky, Sam's little brother. He's only seven.

Mom: Aww!

Rachel: And this is a photo of Sally. She's Sam's big sister. She is 19.

Mom: Oh, she looks smart!

Rachel: This photo is of Ronaldo. He's Sam's friend from school.

Mom: And this girl? Who is she?

Rachel: That's Rebecca. Sam's cousin. She's from America.

Mom: They're lovely photos, Rachel.

UNIT 8

8.8 ex: Those books are mine.

8.8.1 That dog is yours.

8.8.2 These sandwiches are Dan's.

8.8.3 That bag is hers.

8.8.4 Those sandwiches are ours.

8.8.5 That purse is Stacey's.

8.8.6 This key is his.

8.8.7 This newspaper is theirs.

8.8.8 That necklace is Linda's.

8.8.9 Those children are ours.

UNIT 10

10.8 ex: Hi. My name's Pete. I work on a farm with lots of animals. I'm a farmer.

10.8.1 Hi, I'm Simon and I work outside. I'm a gardener and I work with plants.

10.8.2 Hello. My name's Sue. I'm a teacher. I work with children and I teach French and Spanish.

10.8.3 I'm John. I'm a doctor and I work with patients in a hospital.

10.8.4 My name is Alberto. I work in an Italian restaurant and I am a waiter.

10.8.5 I'm Susan. And this is Pam. We work together in a beauty salon. We're hairdressers.

10.8.6 Hello! My name is Douglas. I'm an actor and I work in the theater.

10.8.7 Hello. I'm Danny. I work outside on a construction site. I'm a contractor. It gets very cold here sometimes!

UNIT 11

11.2 ex: A: Hi. Have you got the time?

B: Yes. It's a quarter to six.

11.2.1

A: Excuse me, sir. Do you have the time?

B: Sure. It's a quarter after eight.

11.2.2

A: Hello. Do you know what time it is?

B: Erm. Yep. It's half past eight.

11.2.3

A: Excuse me. Do you know what time it is?

B: It's quarter past eleven.

11.2.4
A: Hello. Have you got the time?
B: It's nine twenty.

11.2.5
A: When do you go to bed?
B: I go to bed at eleven o'clock.

11.2.6
Friend: Hi, Sarah! Do you know what time it is?
Sarah: It's a quarter after seven.

11.2.7
A: Excuse me. Do you have the time?
B: Yes. It's three twenty-five.

11.2.8
A: When did you have breakfast today?
B: I had breakfast at quarter to ten.

11.2.9
Friend: Hi, Jake! Do you know what time it is?
Jake: Sure. It's six twenty-eight.

11.2.10 Ali wakes up at half past five.

11.2.11 Ali goes to bed at ten o'clock.

11.2.12
A: Hello! Have you got the time?
B: Ah, yes. It's almost two thirty.

11.2.13
A: Excuse me. Do you know what time it is?
B: It's a quarter after eight.

UNIT 14

14.7.1 Hi. I'm Kate. I'm a teacher and I work every day from 9am to 5pm. It's hard work, but I go to the gym on Friday. It helps me to relax.

14.7.2 Hello. My name's Paul. I'm a farmer and I work with animals. I work every day from 6am to 9pm. I'm very busy. But I play soccer most weekends with my friends.

14.7.3 I'm Jane. I'm a nurse. I work three days a week, from Wednesday to Friday. On the weekend, I go to a restaurant with my boyfriend, Dan.

14.7.4 Hi there! I'm Sally. I'm a student. I get up at 8am from Monday to Thursday to go to college. On Saturdays, I go swimming with my friends.

14.7.5 My name is Eric. I'm an actor and I work at the theater three times a week. I work on Thursdays, Fridays, and Saturdays. On Sundays, I relax and read the newspaper.

14.7.6 I'm Claire and I'm a waitress. I work in a restaurant from Tuesday to Sunday, and I work late from 6pm to 11pm. On Mondays, I play tennis with my friend, Paul.

UNIT 15

15.3.1 My name's Cath and I'm 26 years old. I work in a hospital, but I'm not a doctor. I'm a nurse and I work with sick children every day.

15.3.2 I'm Joe and I'm an actor. I work in a theater. I'm 50 years old. I live with my wife, Anne and our three cats in our small house in the country.

15.3.3 My name's Miguel and I'm a mailman. I live in New York. It's a really big city! Some people think I'm from Spain, but I'm not Spanish. I come from Argentina.

15.3.4 My name's Pete and I'm 24 years old. I work in a restaurant, but I'm not a waiter. I'm a chef and I cook Italian food from Monday to Friday.

UNIT 16
16.6
Julie: Hi, I'm Julie. I work in the museum in the town center. It's an interesting job and I meet lots of people. My work starts at 10am, so I don't get up early. I usually get up at 8am. I work from Tuesday to Friday. I don't work on Mondays, because the museum is closed. Most days I have lunch with my friends. I work with nice people, and I play tennis with my best friend Sally on Thursday evenings. I get home at 8pm. I eat my dinner and then I watch TV before I go to bed.

UNIT 18
18.4
Jane: Hi there.
Bob: Hello! Are you Jane, the new teacher?
Jane: Yes, I am. Nice to meet you!
Bob: I'm Bob. Nice to meet you.
Jane: What do you teach, Bob?
Bob: I'm an English teacher. What about you? »

Jane: I teach biology.

Bob: You sound Irish, Jane. Are you from Dublin?

Jane: No, I'm not. I'm from Belfast. But my husband Paul is from Dublin.

Bob: And is your husband a teacher here, too?

Jane: No, he isn't. He's a doctor.

Bob: Oh, does he work at the hospital?

Jane: No, he doesn't. He works in a clinic near our house.

Bob: Oh, great! Does he start work early, too?

Jane: No, he doesn't. He starts work at 8:30am.

Bob: My wife works in a bank, so we both have the weekend free. We play a lot of tennis. Do you play tennis, Jane?

Jane: No, I don't. I go to the movies a lot, though.

UNIT 19

19.3

Greg: Let me tell you a bit about my family. Well, there's my grandmother. Her name is Ellie and she's the oldest member of our family. She's 84 years old. She lives in my town near the supermarket.

My mom and dad are called Sharon and Phil. Sharon works in the school on Elm Road and she's a receptionist. My dad, Phil, works in a factory. They make vacuum cleaners there.

I have two sisters. Claire is 21 and Samantha is 19. Claire's a student at the local college, and Samantha works in a beauty salon. And me? I'm a student, too. I study history. I love it, and I want to be a teacher one day.

UNIT 21

21.4.1 I live in a big town called Brookfield. There's a hospital and a hotel. There are three schools and a supermarket near my house. There is a good restaurant, but there isn't a movie theater.

21.4.2 My town's called Alderson. There's a bus station, but there isn't an airport. There are two hotels and a library. There is an old castle, but there aren't any bars or cafés, so it's a little boring.

21.4.3 I live in Barnwell. It's a beautiful town. There's a castle and a church. There is one café, but there aren't any restaurants. There is a museum. My sister works there on the weekend.

21.4.4 I live in Allerton. There is an airport and a train station here. There are two factories and there is a big supermarket. There are no restaurants, but there is a nice café. I go there in the evening.

21.4.5 I live in Weldon. There is a big factory. I work there. There are two cafés near the post office and there is a movie theater, too. There isn't a museum or a church but there is a swimming pool.

21.6

Gordon: Hi, I'm Gordon. I live in Melcome in Canada. There's a town hall and two churches in my town, and there are three schools, too. I'm a teacher and work in a primary school. There is a beautiful park in the center and a small café. I go there in the evening. Melcome is an exciting town: there are two cinemas and a theater. I love the theater! My wife is a doctor and works in the hospital near my house. My son is a police officer and works at the police station.

There aren't any castles in Melcome. It's a very modern city. But there are three new hotels near the airport.

UNIT 22

22.8

James: My name's James. I live on a farm. There are two towns near my home: Stonehill and Eastford. I visit them in the evening with my friends.

Stonehill is a new town, but it has an interesting museum. I go there on the weekend. There are lots of stores and there's a wonderful French restaurant in the center, and I often go there with my girlfriend. There are some great bars, too, but there aren't any theaters.

Eastford is really small and is very old. There's a castle and two churches in the center. There aren't any restaurants in Eastford, but there's a nice café. It's very quiet. There are some nice stores. I sometimes buy a present for my girlfriend there. In the evening you can go to the theater. It's tiny, but it's a lot of fun.

UNIT 23

23.7 ex: A: Is there a theater in Greendale?

B: Yes. Turn left and the theater is on your right across from the church.

23.7.1

A: Excuse me. Where's Franco's restaurant?
B: OK, take the third road on the left. The restaurant is on the right next to the bank.

23.7.2

A: Excuse me. Could you tell where the university is?
B: Sure. Go straight ahead and it's the fourth road on the right. The university is on the left.

23.7.3

A: Excuse me. Where's the supermarket?
B: Turn right, then take the first left. The supermarket is on the left next to the castle.

23.7.4

A: Excuse me. How do I get to Jean-Paul's café?
B: Go straight ahead. The café is on the corner next to the church.

23.7.5

A: Could you tell me where the hotel is?
B: Sure. Go straight ahead and take the second road on your right. It's across from the park.

23.7.6

A: Do you know where the museum is?
B: Yeah, it's next to the town hall. Go straight ahead and take the third left.

23.7.7

A: Excuse me. Is the hospital near here?
B: Yes it is. It's behind the park. Turn right, then take the second left. The hospital is on the corner on the left.

23.7.8

A: Excuse me. How do I get to the café?
B: Turn right. Go past the hotel and the café is on the left.

UNIT 24

24.2 ex: There is a castle and a mosque in my town. They're beautiful.

24.2.1 Newtown has a library and a restaurant.

24.2.2 There's a school and a hospital in Fulchester.

24.2.3 My mom goes to the bank and the supermarket once a week.

24.2.4 I work in two places: a restaurant on Monday evenings and a movie theater on Wednesdays.

24.2.5 There's a museum and a church in my town.

UNIT 25

25.5

Kirsty: My name's Kirsty. I live and work in Braemore. It's a small town in the mountains in Scotland. There are lots of trees and a few lakes near my town. It's beautiful here.

In the center of my town, there are a few old buildings. There's a beautiful church and an old castle. There are lots of hotels and cafes, too. Braemore is very popular with tourists. Lots of people come for a weekend break.

I work in a bar in a large hotel. It's horrible. It's very crowded every weekend and I'm very busy. But when I have some free time, I go to a café with my friends.

UNIT 26

26.2 ex: My name is Leo. I work in an office, so I use a computer every day.

26.2.1 I'm Rick. I live in Cornwall and I work outside. That's because I'm a farmer. I have more than 200 cows.

26.2.2 My name's Mary Lou. I live in Tennessee and I work with children every day, because I'm a teacher.

26.2.3 My name's Carl. I go to the library every day because I'm a student. I'm studying chemistry.

26.2.4 I'm Sally. I get up at 6am because I go to the gym in the morning, before I go to work at the gallery.

26.2.5 My name is Pete and I work in the theater on Park Road. I'm an actor and I have been in many plays.

26.2.6 I'm Michael. I can't go to work today because I have the flu.

26.2.7 I'm Sana. I work in a restaurant in New York because I'm a chef.

UNIT 28

28.7 ex: John's sister has got a cat.
28.7.1 Our town has an old church.
28.7.2 Adam and I have got two daughters.
28.7.3 Sally and Jonathan have a new car.
28.7.4 My friend Sam's got a computer.
28.7.5 Our house has got three rooms.

UNIT 29

29.3 ex: John has a new kitchen. It's quite large and it's in the basement of his house. He has a big refrigerator. You know, John loves cooking.

29.3.1 Claudia has a really good oven. She loves baking cakes.

29.3.2 Paul has a toaster. He makes a lot of toast!

29.3.3 Jenny has a kettle in her office. She can make a cup of tea when she wants one.

29.3.4 Colin has a new washing machine. His mom's very happy, because he doesn't use hers any more.

29.3.5 Roberto has lots of plates and bowls in the cupboards in his kitchen.

UNIT 31

31.5

Kate: Hey, Steve. I'm just doing the shopping list. What do we need this week?

Steve: Good idea, Kate. Let me see. I want to make a cake. We've got three bags of flour in the cupboard! But one bag of sugar. Get me another bag of sugar, please.

Kate: OK. I thought we could make a pizza for dinner tonight.

Steve: We don't have any tomatoes. Can you buy two tins of tomatoes? And we've only got one block of cheese, so please buy some more. Oh, and we've got one carton of juice. Can you get some orange juice?

Kate: Juice, OK. Anything else?

Steve: Well, we need some more fruit. We've only got two oranges. So let's get five more oranges, and six bananas.

Kate: And some apples?

Steve: No, we've got lots of apples.

Kate: OK. We need some coffee, so I'll get two packets. Oh, I don't have any chocolate, so I'll buy two bars of milk chocolate.

Steve: Can you think of anything else?

Kate: Yes, we need some vegetables. We have a lot of onions, but we don't have any other vegetables. I'll buy 500 grams of carrots and some tomatoes.

Steve: Do we have any rice?

Kate: Ooh, no, we haven't. I'll get a bag of rice as well.

UNIT 32

32.4

Bruce: I'm hungry. Let's make a sandwich. Do we have any bread?

Shelley: Let me see. Yes, we do.

Bruce: And some butter?

Shelley: I'm sorry. We don't have enough butter.

Bruce: So, shall we make a pizza, then? You've got a recipe, haven't you?

Shelley: Yes, I have.

Bruce: Right. So, we need some flour. How much flour have we got?

Shelley: Let me see. We've got four bags.

Bruce: That's too many. We only need two.

Shelley: Great. So, here are two bags.

Bruce: What else? Some salt. Do we have any salt?

Shelley: We've got seven ounces of salt.

Bruce: That's too much! We only need one ounce.

Shelley: Brilliant. Now we need some tomatoes, so let's have a look.... 10 ounces. Is that enough?

Bruce: That's not enough. We need 20 ounces.

Shelley: Oh, dear! And what about the cheese?

Bruce: We need six ounces.

Shelley: We've got about seven.

Bruce: OK, that's enough.

Shelley: What else do we need?

Bruce: Well, we've got lots of ham, so let's make a ham pizza.

Shelley: Great!

UNIT 34

34.5 ex: Ruth: Jane, look at those cardigans there.

Jane: Oh, I don't want a red one, Ruth.

Ruth: There is a black one here.

Jane: But they're all quite short. I need a long black cardigan for work.

Ruth: How about this one here? It's long and black.

Jane: Perfect! Now, do they have it in my size?

34.5.1

Ruth: These T-shirts are nice, aren't they, Jane?

Jane: Yes, they're pretty. But I've got lots of T-shirts already.

Ruth: And they have some nice cotton shirts.

Jane: I don't need a shirt. Do they have any skirts?

Ruth: Yes. There are red ones and blue ones.

Jane: I want a red skirt. Can I find one that fits?

34.5.2

Ruth: I want to buy a present for my mother.

Jane: What about these yellow gloves, Ruth?

Ruth: No. They're too expensive.

Jane: How about a hat?

Ruth: She has so many hats already. Those scarves are nice.

Jane: Yes. And not too expensive.

Ruth: I think I'll get her a red scarf.

34.5.3

Jane: Do you like these boots, Ruth?

Ruth: No, they're not my style. I love these shoes though.

Jane: Yes, they're great. Do you want to get the black ones?

Ruth: No, I have some black shoes already. I prefer the brown ones. Do they have them in size 5?

Jane: Let's see.

34.5.4

Ruth: What do you want to get next, Jane?

Jane: Some jeans.

Ruth: What about these?

Jane: They're great, but I want to get some blue ones. I've already got a pair of black jeans.

Ruth: Right. How about these?

Jane: Yes, they look nice.

34.5.5

Ruth: Hey, Jane. There are some gorgeous coats over here.

Jane: Oh, I don't know. They're black. I want something more colorful.

Ruth: How about these here? They have some lovely red ones here.

Jane: They're very cheap. I want something more expensive.

Ruth: OK then, what about that green one there?

Jane: Yes, I'll try it on.

UNIT 35

35.5 ex: A: I love your shoes! What are they made of?

B: They're leather. From Spain.

35.5.1

A: Do you want to come to our party tonight?

B: Sure, I'll bring some wine and some plastic cups.

35.5.2

A: What a beautiful wooden table you have! Is it old?

B: Yes. It's an antique.

35.5.3

A: That's a nice green glass bottle.

B: Thanks. It's a present for my mom.

35.5.4

A: You've got a new leather jacket, haven't you?

B: No. It's quite old, actually.

35.5.5

A: Are those plastic chairs you have?

B: Yes, they're for the yard.

35.5.6

A: What a nice wool sweater you have!

B: Thanks. My sister made it.

35.5.7 My sister has a wooden table, but she doesn't have any chairs.

35.5.8 When I go shopping, I put my fruit in a paper bag.

35.5.9

A: It's my girlfriend's birthday. What should I buy her?

B: Why don't you get her a wool scarf? She'd like that.

35.5.10 I always carry a plastic bottle with me. I put water in it.

35.5.11

Friend: Claire, do you like my new bag?

Claire: Yes, it's gorgeous. Is it leather?

Friend: Of course! It's a present from Tim.

35.5.12

A: That's a beautiful lamp. Is it made of glass?

B: No, it's metal.

35.5.13

A: We have some new chairs for the kitchen.

B: Are they wooden?

A: No. They're metal.

UNIT 37

37.7 ex: I'm Mark and I work in a bank in London. I often play golf on the weekend. I don't have much time during the week, because I work a lot.

37.7.1 I'm Steven and I love cycling. I often go cycling in France in the summer with my wife.

37.7.2 My name's Max. I do a lot of sports because I like to stay fit. I go running every evening after I get home from work. It helps me relax.

37.7.3 Hi, I'm Ian, and I play soccer twice a week, when I meet up with my old school friends.

37.7.4 I'm Janine. I'm not very sporty. I don't like tennis and I hate running.

37.7.5 My name is Lila. What sports do I like? Well, I go skating with my brother in the winter.

37.7.6 My name's Robbie. I don't do much sport. I'm so busy at work that I don't even go running any more.

37.7.7 I'm Susan. I love fishing. I usually go with my grandson Pete on the weekend.

UNIT 39

39.3 ex: John usually goes running.

39.3.1 Chris never gets up early.

39.3.2 Shelley sometimes goes swimming.

39.3.3 Flo often has tea in the morning.

39.3.4 Sylvester usually goes to bed at 10pm.

39.3.5 Dominic always plays soccer on Fridays.

39.3.6 David often reads a newspaper on Sundays.

UNIT 40

40.2

Shelley: So, tell me a bit about yourself, Doug. What kinds of things do you like?

Doug: Well, Shelley, I love my food. I really like fast food. You know, pizza, hamburgers, and fries. What don't I like?

Well, to be honest, I don't like fruit and I hate salad. How about you?

Shelley: I just love sport. I go running every day, and on the weekend I like playing tennis. I don't like golf, though. I think it's boring.

Doug: Me, too! I'm not great at sport, to be honest. But I love reading history books and listening to classical music. I dislike pop music. Oh, and I hate shopping. What else do you do in your free time?

Shelley: I like going to the cinema, but I don't like scary films. I also love taking photos of my friends and family.

UNIT 42

42.2 ex: Hi, I'm Dave. My favorite type of music is jazz. I listen to it in the morning while I drive to work.

42.2.1 Hello! My name is Jenny. I'm still at school and my favorite subject is math. I want to be an engineer when I grow up.

42.2.2 Hi, I'm Mike and I'm a policeman. My favorite day is Friday. Why? Because I'm free on Saturday and don't go to work.

42.2.3 My name's Colin and my favorite color is red. The same color as my favorite football team.

42.2.4 I'm Sally and I love desserts. I like ice cream, but my favorite is, of course, chocolate cake.

42.2.5 Hello, I'm Danny. I like soccer and I really like basketball. But my favorite sport is baseball.

42.2.6 Hi, my name is Clarice. I'm a forest ranger and I work outside. I like summer, but my favorite season is fall, when all the leaves are red and gold.

UNIT 44

44.4 ex: Friend: Hi, Ina. Are you going to James's beach party tomorrow?

Ina: I'm not sure. I can't swim so I won't have much fun.

Friend: Well, you can play beach volleyball instead.

44.4.1

Friend: And where are you going on vacation this summer, Ina?

Ina: I'm going on a horseback riding vacation in Scotland.

Friend: Is that difficult?

Ina: No, it's quite easy. I can ride well.

44.4.2

Friend: Can you speak Mandarin?

Ina: Yes, I can but only a little.

Friend: It's a difficult language to learn. Can you write in Mandarin?

Ina: Oh, no. I can only speak it.

44.4.3

Friend: Can you play tennis?

Ina: No, I'm terrible at it. I can't even hit the ball.

Friend: That's a shame. I'd like to play a game this afternoon.

44.4.4

Friend: Are you musical, Ina?

Ina: Yes, I suppose I am. I can play the piano and the guitar.

Friend: Wow. I can't play any musical instruments.

44.4.5

Ina: How did the kite flying go with your daughter this weekend?

Friend: It didn't go very well. We couldn't get the kite to fly.

Ina: Do you want me to help you next weekend?

Friend: Can you fly a kite?

Ina: Sure I can. I'm really good at that.

UNIT 47

47.5

Kat: What do you want to do later, Pete? Play basketball?

Pete: No thanks, Kat. I'd really like to finish my book.

Kat: No problem. What would you like to do tomorrow?

Pete: Well, I'd really like to go to the park. Do you want to come with me?

Kat: I'd like that. Would you like to go shopping afterwards?

Pete: Yes, I would.

Kat: Great! I want to buy a new dress.

Pete: Do you want to go to see a movie in the evening?

Kat: Actually, I would like to go to a restaurant.

Pete: Oh, good idea. I really want to go to the new Italian restaurant in town.

Kat: I'd like to go there, too. I want to try their spaghetti.

UNIT 48

48.8

A: That's enough about me! Tell me a bit about your grandchildren. How are they?

B: Well, Helen is studying to be a nurse. She'd really like to work in the hospital in the center. She really enjoys the course.

A: And your other granddaughter, Sarah?

B: Sarah is in college in Scotland. She's not sure what she wants to do later, but she thinks she'd really like to be a teacher.

A: And the boys? What are your grandsons doing?

B: Eddie is still at school. He finishes next year, and he wants to get a degree in mathematics. He's a clever one! And then there's Robert. Robert loves music and he'd really like to study it. At the moment he works at a local restaurant where he plays the piano.

A: And Oliver?

B: Oh, Oliver works in the bank on Park Lane. He'd really like to buy a house with his girlfriend, Jane. But it's so expensive. And what about your grandchildren?

Answers

1.1 🔊
1. I'm Natalie.
2. My name's Sue.
3. I'm Ryan.
4. My name's Mia.
5. My name's Amelia.

1.2
A 3 B 1 C 2 D 6 E 4 F 5

1.3 🔊
1. Hi! I am Charlotte.
2. Hi! My name is Charlotte.
3. Hello! I am Charlotte.
4. Hello! My name is Charlotte.
5. Hi! I am Carla.
6. Hi! My name is Carla.
7. Hello! I am Carla.
8. Hello! My name is Carla.
9. Hi! I am Fatima.
10. Hi! My name is Fatima.
11. Hello! I am Fatima.
12. Hello! My name is Fatima.

1.4
1. N-o-a-h A-n-d-e-r-s-o-n
2. M-a-s-o-n H-u-g-h-e-s
3. E-l-i S-a-n-d-e-r-s
4. A-l-i-c-i-a
5. Z-o-e S-p-i-e-g-e-l-m-a-n
6. B-e-n
7. N-o-r-a J-a-m-e-s
8. A-m-i-r A-n-s-a-r-i
9. N-i-n-a E-d-w-a-r-d-s
10. L-u-c-y
11. A-m-a-n S-h-a-r-m-a
12. A-i-d-e-n
13. K-e-i-t-h
14. F-i-o-n-a
15. J-a-m-e-s T-h-o-m-a-s

1.5 🔊
1. My name is Terry, T-e-r-r-y.
2. My last name is Singh, S-i-n-g-h.

3. I'm Mario, M-a-r-i-o.
4. My name is Yasmin Khan, Y-a-s-m-i-n K-h-a-n.
5. I am Jacob, J-a-c-o-b.

2.1 🔊
1. South Korea
2. Thailand
3. Greece
4. Poland
5. Argentina
6. Russia
7. Australia
8. Canada
9. Philippines
10. Pakistan
11. Slovakia
12. Republic of Ireland
13. China
14. Portugal
15. South Africa
16. Brazil
17. Netherlands
18. Spain
19. Czech Republic
20. Singapore
21. Egypt
22. Mongolia
23. United Kingdom
24. France
25. Mexico
26. India
27. United States of America
28. Japan
29. Indonesia
30. United Arab Emirates
31. New Zealand
32. Germany
33. Austria
34. Switzerland

3.1 🔊
1. 85 2. 21 3. 90 4. 17 5. 84 6. 62
7. 47 8. 50 9. 71 10. 12 11. 33

3.2 🔊
1. Chloe is thirty-one years old.
2. Heidi is fifty-two years old.
3. Zach is sixteen years old.
4. Charlie is ten years old.
5. Marcel is eighty years old.
6. Claire is twenty-one years old.
7. Dan is thirty-six years old.
8. Eleanor is twenty-eight years old.
9. Rebecca is forty-three years old.

3.3 🔊
1. I am twenty-three years old.
2. I am thirty-two years old.
3. I am sixty-eight years old.
4. Dan is twenty-three years old.
5. Dan is thirty-two years old.
6. Dan is sixty-eight years old.
7. You are twenty-three years old.
8. You are thirty-two years old.
9. You are sixty-eight years old.

3.4 🔊
1. Abe **is** 72 years old. She **is** Japanese.
2. Mia and Leo **are** 12. They **are** from Italy.
3. Chantal **is** 66 years old. She **is** French.
4. Amir and Aamna **are** 90 years old. They **are** from Pakistan.
5. I **am** 24 years old. I **am** Irish.
6. Max **is** 47 years old. He **is** German.
7. We **are** 38 years old. We **are** from New Zealand.
8. My sister **is** 4 years old. She **is** from Canada.

4.1 🔊
1. grandfather
2. father
3. uncle
4. sister
5. son
6. daughter
7. grandson
8. granddaughter

4.2 🔊
1. cat
2. chicken

③ rabbit
④ tortoise
⑤ parrot
⑥ dog
⑦ fish
⑧ snake
⑨ pig
⑩ horse
⑪ guinea pig

05

5.1 🔊
❶ **Their** dog is called Beth.
❷ **His** tortoise is 50 years old.
❸ **My** cat is called Sam.
❹ **Our** lion is from Kenya.
❺ **Your** rabbit eats grass.
❻ Here is **its** bed.
❼ **Their** snake is called Sid.
❽ Buster is **my** monkey.
❾ **Your** parrot is from Venezuela.
❿ **Her** cat is called Tabatha.
⓫ **Their** monkey is from Morocco.
⓬ **Her** pig lives on a farm.
⓭ **His** horse is called Prancer.
⓮ **Our** chicken lives in the garden.

5.2 🔊
❶ Fido is **my** dog.
❷ Cookie is **his** cat.
❸ It is **our** chicken.
❹ Ziggy is **your** parrot.
❺ Hiss is **their** snake.
❻ Max is **our** monkey.
❼ It is **her** rabbit.
❽ Ed is **my** horse.
❾ Rex is **your** dog.
❿ Nemo is **her** fish.
⓫ It is **our** sheep.

5.3 🔊
❶ **This** is her rabbit.
❷ **This** is its ball.
❸ **That** is our dog.
❹ **This** is his snake.
❺ **That** is my horse.

5.4 🔊
❶ Their fish is called Bob.
❷ This is their cow.

③ His snake is called Harold.
④ Her cat is 12 years old.
⑤ Barney is our rabbit.

5.5 🔊
1. This is her cat.
2. This is her parrot.
3. This is their cat.
4. This is their parrot.
5. This is my cat.
6. This is my parrot.
7. That is her cat.
8. That is her parrot.
9. That is their cat.
10. That is their parrot.
11. That is my cat.
12. That is my parrot.

06

6.1 🔊
❶ Joe and Greg's dog
❷ Dolly's granddaughters
❸ Sue's house
❹ Pete and Aziz's snake

6.2
❶ Arthur is **Sam's grandfather.**
❷ Frank is **Sam's father.**
❸ Charlotte is **Sam's mother.**
❹ Micky is **Sam's brother.**
❺ Sally is **Sam's sister.**
❻ Ronaldo is **Sam's friend.**
❼ Rebecca is **Sam's cousin.**

6.3
❶ True ❷ False ❸ False
❹ True ❺ False

6.4 🔊
❶ That's my grandparents' car.
❷ These are Pete and Omar's cats.
❸ I am Sally's granddaughter.
❹ Where is your parents' house?
❺ Samantha is Barry's new wife.

6.5 🔊
❶ Sooty is **my brothers'** cat.
❷ They are **Tammy's** parents.
❸ This is our **children's** snake.
❹ My **parents'** house is small.

07

7.1 🔊
❶ notebook
❷ sunglasses
❸ keys
❹ pen
❺ necklace
❻ newspaper
❼ ID card
❽ letter
❾ toothbrush
❿ hairbrush
⓫ bottle of water
⓬ laptop
⓭ earphones
⓮ pencil
⓯ dictionary
⓰ apple
⓱ book
⓲ tablet
⓳ mirror
⓴ coins
㉑ passport
㉒ magazine
㉓ camera
㉔ glasses
㉕ map
㉖ umbrella
㉗ sandwich

08

8.1 🔊
❶ **These** are my mom's glasses.
❷ **Those** are Samantha's keys.
❸ **This** is Tom's umbrella.
❹ **This** is my dog.
❺ **Those** are Pete's books.
❻ **That** is your newspaper.
❼ **These** are my tickets.
❽ **These** are Marge's earrings.
❾ **These** are his daughters.
❿ **That** is my teacher.
⓫ **That** is your watch.

8.2
❶ This is my letter.
❷ These are my purses.

3 That is Greg's key.

4 Those are my cats.

5 This is my sister's pencil.

6 Those are your dictionaries.

7 These are Dan's houses.

8 That is Stan's book.

9 That is my brother.

8.3 🔊

1 pencils

2 fishes / fish

3 brothers

4 diaries

5 necklaces

6 brushes

7 watches

8 boxes

9 dictionaries

10 sisters

11 umbrellas

12 laptops

8.4 🔊

1 brushes

2 boxes

3 dictionaries

4 dogs

5 notebooks

6 toothbrushes

7 books

8 pencils

9 letters

10 newspapers

11 glasses

12 passports

13 magazines

8.5

1 three sandwiches

2 two necklaces

3 four bags

4 three toothbrushes

5 two diaries / planners

6 two cats

7 one apple

8.6 🔊

1 his

2 its

3 hers

4 yours

5 theirs

6 ours

8.7 🔊

1 This dog is his.

2 Those books are mine.

3 That fish is yours.

4 These bags are theirs.

5 These boxes are ours.

8.8

1 That dog is yours.

2 These sandwiches are Dan's.

3 That bag is hers.

4 Those sandwiches are ours.

5 That purse is Stacey's.

6 This key is his.

7 This newspaper is theirs.

8 That necklace is Linda's.

9 Those children are ours.

8.9 🔊

1 **These** are my books.

2 **This** is your dog.

3 **These** are her bags.

4 **These** are their boxes.

5 **This** is my toothbrush.

6 **This** is his diary.

7 **This** is your apple.

8 **These** are my apples.

9 **These** are your glasses.

10 **These** are Kevin's keys.

11 **This** is my dad's car.

8.10

DETERMINERS: **your**, **his**, **my**
PRONOUNS: **hers**, **mine**

09

9.1 🔊

1 pilot

2 fire fighter

3 gardener

4 driver

5 electrician

6 actor

7 nurse

8 farmer

9 chef

10 receptionist

11 businesswoman

12 police officer

13 dentist

14 vet

15 teacher

16 businessman

17 mechanic

18 waiter

19 engineer

20 cleaner

21 artist

22 hairdresser

23 waitress

24 construction worker

25 doctor

26 sales assistant

27 judge

10

10.1

1 He / She is a doctor.

2 You are teachers.

3 I am a hairdresser.

4 We are mechanics.

5 You are a cleaner.

6 They are chefs.

7 He / She is an actor.

8 They are vets.

9 I am a police officer.

10 You are farmers.

11 You are a waitress.

12 We are gardeners.

13 I am an artist.

10.2 🔊

1 I **am an** actor.

2 He **is a** teacher.

3 He **is a** chef.

4 You **are an** engineer.

5 We **are** hairdressers.

6 They **are** farmers.

7 You **are a** vet.

8 I **am a** waiter.

9 She **is a** nurse.

10.3 🔊

1 I **am** a vet.

2 She **is** a businesswoman.

3 We **are** doctors.

4 They **are** teachers.

5 He **is** a mechanic.

6 I **am** a driver.

7 We **are** receptionists.

8 They **are** waitresses.
9 She **is** a police officer.
10 I **am** a judge.
11 You **are** a nurse.
12 We **are** farmers.
13 She **is** a sales assistant.
14 I **am** a chef.

10.4 ◀))
1 laboratory
2 restaurant
3 garden
4 hospital
5 school

10.5 ◀))
1 He works **in** a doctor's office.
2 We work **on** a farm.
3 My dad works **on** a building site.
4 My sister works **in** a café.
5 We work **in** people's gardens.
6 Dan works **in** a hospital.
7 I work **in** a restaurant.
8 We work **in** a school.
9 Chris works **in** a supermarket.

10.6 ◀))
1 Abby **is a nurse**. She **works in a hospital**.
2 Julie **is an engineer**. She **works on a construction site**.
3 Simon **is a gardener**. He **works in a park**.
4 Adam **is a police officer**. He **works in a police station**.
5 Max **is a farmer**. He **works on a farm**.
6 Carol **is a hairdresser**. She **works in a beauty salon**.

10.7 ◀))
1 Sam is a **doctor** and she works with **patients**.
2 Gabriella is a **chef** and she works with **food**.
3 Dan is a **vet** and he works with **animals**.
4 John is a **farmer** and he works with **crops**.
5 Tom is an **actor** and he works in a **theater**.

10.8
1 gardener
2 teacher
3 doctor
4 waiter

5 hairdressers
6 actor
7 contractor

11

11.1 ◀))
1 It's four thirty.
2 It's seven fifty.
3 It's midnight.
4 It's a quarter after six.
5 It's half past eight.
6 It's three thirty.
7 It's a quarter to nine.
8 It's five forty-five.

11.2
1 08:15
2 08:30
3 11:15
4 09:20
5 11:00
6 07:15
7 03:25
8 09:45
9 06:28
10 05:30
11 10:00
12 02:30
13 08:15

11.3 ◀))
1 11:15
2 11:00
3 8:24
4 3:30
5 2:45
6 5:25
7 3:49
8 2:15
9 9:00
10 7:45
11 11:30
12 9:25
13 10:15
14 11:20
15 1:55
16 6:45
17 6:45

11.4 ◀))
1 It's a quarter to ten. / It's nine forty-five.
2 It's four o'clock.
3 It's ten twenty.
4 It's half past eleven. / It's eleven thirty.
5 It's three forty-seven.
6 It's a quarter past three. / It's three fifteen.
7 It's half past six. / It's six thirty.
8 It's eight twenty-two.
9 It's one twenty-five.

12

12.1 ◀))
1 buy groceries
2 take a bath
3 have lunch
4 clear the table
5 start work
6 wash your face
7 get up
8 cook dinner
9 brush your hair
10 leave work
11 finish work
12 brush your teeth
13 go home
14 have dinner
15 go to school
16 get dressed
17 go to bed
18 take a shower
19 wake up
20 iron a shirt
21 dawn
22 day
23 dusk
24 night
25 do the dishes
26 have breakfast
27 walk the dog

13

13.1 ◀))
1 Marion has a shower at 6:45am.
2 Marion has breakfast at 7am.
3 Marion brushes her teeth at 7:20am.

④ Marion goes to work at 7:30am.

⑤ Marion gets the bus at 7:45am.

⑥ Marion gets to work at 8:30am.

⑦ Marion leaves work at 5pm.

13.2 🔊

① I **wake** up at 6:30am.

② He **gets** up at 6am.

③ She **has** a shower at 7am.

④ They **have** cereal for breakfast.

⑤ He **has** a shower before breakfast.

⑥ She **leaves** home at 7:15am.

⑦ The bus **goes** every half hour.

⑧ I **get** to work at 8:30am.

⑨ He **starts** work at 9am.

⑩ She **takes** an hour for lunch.

⑪ I **go** to the sandwich shop for lunch.

⑫ They **eat** lunch in the canteen.

⑬ He **finishes** work at 5pm.

⑭ They **go** home on the bus.

⑮ He **washes** his car every weekend.

⑯ I **watch** TV after dinner.

⑰ They **go** to bed at 11pm.

⑱ He **sleeps** for eight hours.

13.3 🔊

① He **has**

② It **starts**

③ He **leaves**

④ She **gets up**

⑤ It **goes**

⑥ She **wakes up**

⑦ He **washes**

⑧ She **watches**

⑨ It **finishes**

13.4 🔊

① He **gets** up at 6:30am.

② He **has** breakfast at 7am.

③ She **leaves** home at 8am.

④ I **drive** to work.

⑤ I **have** lunch in the park.

⑥ I **work** eight hours every day.

⑦ He **goes** to bed at 10:30pm.

13.5 🔊

① goes

② washes

③ wakes

④ gets

⑤ watches

⑥ leaves

⑦ has

⑧ finishes

14

14.1 🔊

① I go to the movies **on** the weekend.

② Joe starts work at 6pm **on** Mondays.

③ You watch TV **in** the afternoon.

④ Harry plays tennis **on** Wednesdays.

⑤ Lin goes swimming **in** the evening.

⑥ Alex goes fishing **on** the weekend.

⑦ He eats lunch at 1pm **on** Fridays.

⑧ Sam goes to the gym **in** the morning.

14.2 🔊

① I work from Monday to Thursday.

② My sister goes swimming every day.

③ We go to the gym on Saturdays.

④ You read the newspaper on Sundays.

⑤ Peter goes to work on the weekend.

⑥ Jennifer goes to a café on Fridays.

⑦ Sam and Pete work from 9am to 5pm.

14.3 🔊

① Pam works **from** Monday **to** Friday.

② I work at home **on** Thursdays.

③ Tom goes to the cinema **on** Fridays.

④ I play soccer **on / at** the weekend.

⑤ They work **from** Monday **to** Thursday.

⑥ We go to bed at 9pm **on** Mondays.

⑦ Laura goes shopping **on** Tuesdays.

⑧ Peter gets up at 8am **on** Mondays.

⑨ We go the gym **on** Thursdays.

⑩ Gerald reads a book **on / at** the weekend.

⑪ Jane swims **from** Monday **to** Friday.

⑫ John takes a bath **on** Fridays.

⑬ Lizzy starts work at 9am **on** Fridays.

14.4 🔊

① Dan goes to the gym three times a week.

② Sam goes to the cinema twice a week.

③ We go to bed at 11:30pm every day.

④ Joe goes to college five times a week.

⑤ Clarice washes her clothes once a week.

⑥ Jennifer gets up at 10am twice a week.

⑦ We eat dinner at 7pm every day.

14.5 🔊

① Bob **goes swimming** on Thursdays.

② I play tennis **on the weekend / at the weekend**.

③ Jane and Tom go to the gym **three times** a week.

④ Angus works from **Monday to Thursday**.

⑤ I go to the movies **on the weekend / at the weekend**.

⑥ Sam goes to **college on Wednesdays**.

⑦ Jenny gets up **at 7am** every day.

⑧ Peter **works from** Monday to Friday.

⑨ Nina **goes to bed** at 11pm every day.

14.6

① False ② True ③ False ④ True

⑤ False ⑥ True

14.7

Ⓐ 3

Ⓑ 6

Ⓒ 4

Ⓓ 5

Ⓔ 1

Ⓕ 2

14.8

① farmer

② nurse

③ restaurant

④ 8am

⑤ Saturday

⑥ theater

⑦ three days

⑧ waitress

⑨ 6pm

15

15.1 🔊

① Paula is not a teacher.

② We are not from England.

③ This is not my phone.

④ Kirsty is not 18 years old.

⑤ Frank is not my father.

⑥ This is not my purse.

⑦ They are not engineers.

⑧ That is not a salon.

⑨ Kim is not a teacher.

15.2 🔊

① That **is not** a castle.

② They **are not** at school.

③ He **is not** a grandfather.

④ We **are not** engineers.

⑤ She **is not** 70 years old.

⑥ You **are not** French.

⑦ This **is not** my dog.

8 I **am not** a doctor.

9 It **is not** 11 o'clock.

15.3

A 3

B 1

C 2

D 4

15.4

1 Fredo is not a chef.
Fredo isn't a chef.

2 Susie's not my cat.
Susie isn't my cat.

3 My dad is not at work.
My dad's not at work.

4 They are not at the theater.
They aren't at the theater.

15.5

1 True

2 False

3 True

4 True

5 False

15.6 ◀))

1 This **isn't** his umbrella.

2 Pedro **isn't** Spanish.

3 Pete and Terry **aren't** hairdressers.

4 It **isn't** a snake.

5 My cousins **aren't** 21 years old.

6 It **isn't** half past six.

7 **I'm not** your friend.

15.7

1 True

2 True

3 False

4 True

5 True

6 False

15.8 ◀))

1 I'm a student. I'm not a teacher.

2 I'm 30 years old. I'm not 40.

3 I'm a farmer. I'm not a police officer.

4 I'm French. I'm not English.

5 I'm an uncle. I'm not a father.

6 I'm 18. I'm not 21.

7 I'm a waitress. I'm not a chef.

8 I'm Spanish. I'm not Italian.

15.9 ◀))

1 You're 28. You're not 29.

2 You're a scientist. You're not a gardener.

3 You're Austrian. You're not English.

4 You're a contractor. You're not an actor.

5 You're 16. You're not 18.

6 You're an uncle. You're not a grandfather.

7 You're a mechanic. You're not an engineer.

8 You're a police officer. You're not a firefighter.

15.10 ◀))

1. I'm not at work.

2. I'm not an actor.

3. I'm not American.

4. I'm not 40 years old.

5. You aren't at work.

6. You aren't an actor.

7. You aren't American.

8. You aren't 40 years old.

9. She isn't at work.

10. She isn't an actor.

11. She isn't American.

12. She isn't 40 years old.

16

16.1 ◀))

1 Jane **does not** walk to work.

2 My brother **does not** watch TV.

3 I **do not** read a book in the evening.

4 Frank **does not** work at the museum.

5 They **do not** go dancing on the weekend.

6 We **do not** go to work on Fridays.

7 I **do not** get up at 7:30am.

8 You **do not** have a car.

9 My dad **does not** work in an office.

10 You **do not** have a dog.

11 My sister **does not** work with children.

12 They **do not** live in the country.

13 Freddie **does not** eat meat.

16.2 ◀))

1 Tony doesn't live in New York.

2 Sebastian doesn't work on a farm.

3 My uncle doesn't work in a factory.

4 We don't play soccer on Thursdays.

5 I don't learn German at school.

6 Carlo doesn't work on Mondays.

7 You don't take a bath at night.

16.3

1 Tim does not play tennis.
Tim doesn't play tennis.

2 You do not have a black cat.
You don't have a black cat.

3 Jules does not read a book every day.
Jules doesn't read a book every day.

4 Sam does not work in a restaurant.
Sam doesn't work in a restaurant.

5 They do not play soccer.
They don't play soccer.

6 Emily does not work with animals.
Emily doesn't work with animals.

7 Mel and Greg do not have a car.
Mel and Greg don't have a car.

8 You do not work in a factory.
You don't work in a factory.

16.4 ◀))

1 Chloe **doesn't** play tennis with her friends.

2 You **don't** work outside.

3 Sal and Doug **don't** have a car.

4 We **don't** watch TV at home.

5 Mrs. O'Brien **doesn't** work in an office.

6 You **don't** wake up at 6am.

7 They **don't** eat lunch at 1pm.

8 Virginia **doesn't** speak good English.

9 Trevor **doesn't** live near here.

10 My dad **doesn't** live in Los Angeles.

11 David **doesn't** play chess.

16.5 ◀))

1 Jean doesn't cycle to work.

2 They don't live in the city.

3 Mr. James doesn't go to the theater.

4 He doesn't read a newspaper.

5 My cousins don't have tickets.

6 Sally doesn't go to the gym.

7 Our dog doesn't have a ball.

8 I don't have a laptop.

9 My mom doesn't get up at 7:30am.

10 You don't live in the country.

11 Claude doesn't have a dictionary.

16.6

1 False **2** False **3** True **4** False

5 True **6** False **7** True

16.7

1 Carla **2** Sam **3** Greg **4** Carla

5 Sam **6** Greg **7** Sam **8** Carla

16.8 🔊

1. I don't go swimming.
2. I don't have a car.
3. I don't speak Japanese.
4. Frank doesn't go swimming.
5. Frank doesn't have a car.
6. Frank doesn't speak Japanese.
7. We don't go swimming.
8. We don't have a car.
9. We don't speak Japanese.

17

17.1 🔊

1 Is this his passport?
2 Is it 6 o'clock?
3 Are Doug and Jim hairdressers?
4 Are these my glasses?
5 Is Sally his sister?
6 Are those your letters?
7 Is she a nurse?
8 Is this your snake?
9 Is it 3pm?
10 Is his wife a chef?
11 Are Katie and Jess my friends?

17.2 🔊

1. Are you an actor?
2. Are you a teacher?
3. Are you engineers?
4. Are they engineers?
5. Is she a teacher?
6. Is she an actor?

17.3 🔊

1 **Is** Dorota at school?
2 **Is** this your parrot?
3 **Is** there a bank near here?
4 **Are** you a gardener?
5 **Are** these Jean's keys?
6 **Is** there a castle in your town?
7 **Is** that your bag?
8 **Are** they your cousins?
9 **Are** they from France?
10 **Is** she Sam's sister?
11 **Is** this my burger?
12 **Is** there a church in this town?
13 **Are** those Brooke's shirts?

17.4 🔊

1 Is Paula from Italy?
2 Is it half past two?
3 Is Ronaldo your father?
4 Is there a bank on your street?
5 Are these your dad's glasses?
6 Is this your laptop?
7 Are those Katherine's books?

17.5 🔊

1 **Do** you work in a hospital?
2 **Does** your dog like children?
3 **Do** you get up at 10am on Sundays?
4 **Does** Simone work with children?
5 **Do** they live in the town?
6 **Do** we finish work at 3pm today?
7 **Does** Frank play tennis with Pete?

17.6 🔊

1 **Do** you read a newspaper every day?
2 **Does** he go to bed at 11pm?
3 **Do** they live in a castle?
4 **Does** Pedro come from Bolivia?
5 **Does** she work with children?
6 **Do** Claire and Sam eat lunch at 2pm?
7 **Does** your brother work with animals?
8 **Does** Tim play soccer on Mondays?
9 **Do** they work in a café?
10 **Do** you have a shower in the evening?
11 **Do** we start work at 10am on Thursdays?
12 **Does** Pamela work in a bank?

17.7 🔊

1 Do they work in a museum?
2 Do you work with children?
3 Does Shane live in Sydney?
4 Does John play tennis on Wednesdays?
5 Do Yves and Marie eat dinner at 6pm?
6 Does Seth work in a post office?

17.8

1 No 2 No 3 Yes 4 Yes
5 Yes 6 No 7 Yes

17.9 🔊

1 **Do** you go to a restaurant on Fridays?
2 **Does** Peter live near the museum?
3 **Do** Sam and Doug work with animals?
4 **Does** she get up at 7am on the weekend?
5 **Do** they play tennis in the evening?

18

18.1 🔊

1 Yes, I do.
2 No, they aren't.
3 Yes, it is.
4 Yes, she does.
5 Yes, it is.

18.2 🔊

1 No, **I don't.**
2 Yes, **she is.**
3 No, **he doesn't.**
4 No, **they don't.**
5 Yes, **he is.**

18.3

1 No, she isn't.
2 No, she doesn't.
3 No, it isn't.
4 Yes, she does.
5 No, she doesn't.

18.4

1 True 2 False 3 False 4 True
5 True 6 Not given 7 True

19

19.1 🔊

1 Franco. And yours?
2 I'm fine, thanks.
3 It's half past seven.
4 That's my wife, Vicky.
5 It's across from the bank.
6 It's his birthday.
7 He's the boy with red hair.
8 It's at 3 o'clock.
9 It's on Saturday.
10 I'm twenty-three.

19.2 🔊

1 **Why** does the dog keep barking?
2 **Where** are your parents now?
3 **Who** is your brother?
4 **What** is your name?
5 **When** is Carla's birthday?
6 **Where** is your sister's house?
7 **Which** car is yours?

8 **When** are your exams?
9 **Where** did you park the car?
10 **Why** are you sad?
11 **When** can I go home?
12 **Where** does your brother live?
13 **What** is your first memory?

19.3
1 84 years old
2 Near the supermarket
3 At a school
4 She's a receptionist
5 19

19.4 ◄))
1 Which shirt do you prefer?
2 Where does your son go to college?
3 How do you get to work?
4 Where do you go swimming?
5 What time do you go to bed?
6 When does Jane start work?
7 What do you eat for breakfast?

19.5 ◄))
1 **What** do you study?
2 **Which** do you want?
3 **Which** building is your college?
4 **Where** do you live?
5 **What** time do you wake up?
6 **How** many shirts do you own?
7 **What** do you want for lunch?
8 **When** does the course finish?
9 **What** do you do in the evening?

19.6 ◄))
1 Which school does he go to?
2 Why does Kevin work there?
3 Where does your friend live?
4 Where is your car?
5 What does your brother do?

19.7 ◄))
1 How is your uncle?
2 Which woman is your wife?
3 Where do you work?
4 What time is the meeting?
5 When do you finish work tonight?

19.8 ◄))
1. Where does he play soccer?
2. Where does Jane play soccer?
3. Where do you play soccer?
4. Where does he live?

5. Where does Jane live?
6. Where do you live?
7. When does he play soccer?
8. When does he finish work?
9. When do you play soccer?
10. When do you finish work?
11. When does Jane play soccer?
12. When does Jane finish work?

19.9
1 Blois
2 Janet
3 Near the castle
4 French bread
5 In a café
6 Explore the old town
7 About 1,000 years old
8 Some beautiful paintings

20

20.1 ◄))
1 school
2 police station
3 supermarket
4 bridge
5 hotel
6 here
7 post office
8 mosque
9 town
10 park
11 library
12 airport
13 there
14 hospital
15 pharmacy
16 bank
17 train station
18 factory
19 bar
20 near
21 castle
22 bus station
23 restaurant
24 office building
25 swimming pool
26 café
27 far

21

21.1 ◄))
1 **There is** a station.
2 **There is** a swimming pool.
3 **There are** two theaters.
4 **There is** a factory.
5 **There are** two parks.
6 **There are** three cafés.

21.2 ◄))
1 There **isn't** a restaurant.
2 There **aren't** any schools.
3 There **isn't** a post office.
4 There **aren't** any cafés.
5 There **aren't** any bars.
6 There **isn't** a train station.
7 There **isn't** a library.
8 There **aren't** any supermarkets.
9 There **aren't** any parks.
10 There **isn't** a town hall.

21.3 ◄))
1. There is a hotel.
2. There is no hotel.
3. There are three parks.
4. There are no parks.
5. There aren't any parks.
6. There are three books.
7. There are no books.
8. There aren't any books.

21.4
A 3
B 2
C 1
D 4
E 5

21.5 ◄))
1 There isn't a school.
2 There aren't two churches.
3 There isn't a café.
4 There isn't a library.
5 There aren't two airports.
6 There aren't three hotels.
7 There aren't two parks.
8 There isn't a town hall.

21.6
1 churches
2 primary school

3 café
4 hospital
5 police officer

21.7 🔊
1 There is a supermarket.
2 There aren't any restaurants.
3 There are no hotels.
4 There are three schools.
5 There is a bus station.

21.8
1 False
2 True
3 False
4 False
5 True
6 False
7 True

21.9 🔊
1 There are three stores.
2 There are two castles.
3 There isn't a church.
4 There is a hospital.
5 There isn't a post office.

22

22.1 🔊
1 **The** new doctor is called Hilary.
2 Sammy is **a** nurse.
3 There is **a** bank downtown.
4 Is there **a** hospital near here?
5 **The** gym is near Sam's house.
6 There is **a** new café in town.
7 **The** hotel on Elm Lane is nice.
8 **The** new teacher is good.
9 There's **an** old theater in town.

22.2 🔊
1 I have **a** sister and **a** brother.
2 There is **a** library on Queens Road.
3 I bought **an** apple and **an** orange.
4 Is there **a** bank near here?
5 There is **a** café at the bus station.
6 My dad is **an** engineer.
7 There is **a** cell phone on the table.

22.3
Dear Bob and Sally,
We are in Glenmuir, **a** quiet town in Scotland. There's **a** castle and **a** cathedral here. They're beautiful, and **the** castle is really old. There are **some** interesting stores, which we visit every day. We also have **a** new friend here. He's called Alfonso and he works as **a** waiter in **the** Italian restaurant next to **the** shopping mall. He's great!
Jane

22.4 🔊
1 Are there **any** factories in your town?
2 Is there **a** gym downtown?
3 Are there **any** pencils in your bag?
4 Is there **an** old church on Station Road?
5 Is there **a** hospital in the town?
6 Is there **a** salon near here?
7 Is there **an** apple in the basket?
8 Are there **any** restaurants in your town?
9 Is there **a** library downtown?
10 Are there **any** books on the table?
11 Is there **a** café nearby?
12 Is there **a** cathedral in that town?
13 Is there **a** bank near the supermarket?
14 Are there **any** kittens here?
15 Is there **a** school in this neighborhood?

22.5 🔊
1 Is there a supermarket near here?
2 There are some cafés on Beech Road.
3 There are some horses on Frank's farm.
4 There are some hotels near the airport.

22.6 🔊
1 Is **there a** museum?
2 Are **there any** cafés?
3 Are **there any** parks near here?
4 Is **there a** mosque in the town?
5 Is **there an** airport in Saltforth?
6 Are **there any** factories in Halford?
7 Is **there a** castle in your town?

22.7 🔊
1 Yes, **there are**.
2 No, **there isn't**.
3 Yes, **there are**.
4 No, **there isn't**.
5 Yes, **there is**.
6 No, **there aren't**.
7 Yes, **there are**.

22.8
1 Stonehill
2 Museum
3 Lots
4 French
5 None
6 Two
7 Some

23

23.1 🔊
1 put
2 read
3 work
4 start
5 eat
6 have
7 stop
8 wake up
9 run
10 come
11 be

23.2 🔊
1 present simple
2 imperative
3 present simple
4 imperative
5 imperative
6 imperative
7 present simple
8 present simple
9 imperative

23.3 🔊
1 Go straight ahead. The swimming pool is opposite the station.
2 Take the second left. The school is opposite the factory.
3 Turn right and take the first left. The church is opposite the hotel.
4 Take the third left and go straight ahead. The theater is on the right.

23.4 🔊
1 Go past the house.
2 Take the second right.
3 Go straight ahead.
4 Turn left.
5 Take the third right.

23.5 🔊
① on the left
② opposite
③ on the right
④ behind
⑤ on the corner

23.6 🔊
① Don't go straight ahead.
② Don't come with me.
③ Don't take the first left.
④ Don't turn left at the intersection.
⑤ Don't read this daily planner.

23.7
Ⓐ 5 Ⓑ 2 Ⓒ 6 Ⓓ 4 Ⓔ 9
Ⓕ 8 Ⓖ 3 Ⓗ 7

23.8 🔊
① The museum is **next to** the library.
② The restaurant is **opposite** the store.
③ The hospital is **in front of** the theater.
④ The post office is **behind** the school.

24

24.1 🔊
① My cousin lives and **works in Los Angeles.**
② I play soccer and **basketball in the evening.**
③ There's a library and **a bookstore in my town.**
④ I eat two eggs and **a banana for breakfast.**
⑤ Pete's uncle and **aunt live in Arizona.**
⑥ I read a book and **watch TV on the weekend.**

24.2
① restaurant
② hospital
③ supermarket
④ movie theater
⑤ church

24.3 🔊
① Three chefs and four waiters work in my hotel.
② There's a park, a café, and a theater in Pella.

③ I have one aunt, two sisters, and a niece.
④ Ben eats breakfast, lunch, and dinner.
⑤ I play tennis and soccer.
⑥ We have a dog and a cat.
⑦ I read a book and take a bath on Sundays.
⑧ Jen speaks French, Spanish, and Japanese.
⑨ Pete has two dogs and a cat.

24.4 🔊
① This is my brother and these are my sisters.
② I speak English, but I don't speak French.
③ I play video games and I watch TV.
④ I have one uncle, but I don't have any aunts.
⑤ There are two stores and three hotels.
⑥ I eat lunch every day, but I don't eat breakfast.
⑦ There's a hotel, but there isn't a store.
⑧ I have a sandwich and an apple.
⑨ This is my house, but these aren't my keys.
⑩ Those are Sarah's magazines and that is her ID card.
⑪ This phone is Joe's, but this laptop isn't.

24.5 🔊
① There's a library, a store, **and** a café.
② There's a castle and a church **but** there isn't a museum.
③ Pete eats apples **but** doesn't eat bananas.
④ Greg reads magazines **and** a newspaper.
⑤ I have a calendar **and** a notebook.
⑥ He goes swimming **but** he doesn't play soccer.

24.6 🔊
① Meg likes this restaurant **but** she doesn't like that café.
② There are two schools **but** there isn't a library in my town.
③ I have a pen, a notebook, **and** a calendar in my bag.
④ My sister goes to the gym on Mondays **and** Thursdays.
⑤ Pedro works in a school **but** he isn't a teacher.

25

25.1 🔊
① I am a busy man.
② There is a new restaurant.
③ My friend is a beautiful woman.
④ We have a very old cat.
⑤ These are my new clothes.

25.2
① good
② beautiful
③ wonderful
④ busy
⑤ interesting
⑥ old
⑦ large

25.3 🔊
① The children are small.
   They are small.
② The waiter is good.
   He is good.
③ The dog is big.
   It is big.
④ The town is quiet.
   It is quiet.

25.4 🔊
① new
② large
③ bad
④ beautiful
⑤ old
⑥ slow
⑦ easy

25.5
① False ② True ③ False ④ True
⑤ False ⑥ True

25.6 🔊
① **The** sea **is** blue **and the** sun **is** hot.
② **The** beach **is** busy **and the** hotels **are** ugly.
③ **The** city **is** old **and the** buildings **are** beautiful.
④ **The** restaurant **is** good **and the** waiter **is** friendly.
⑤ **The** countryside **is** beautiful **and the** mountains **are** large.

6 The town **is** small **and the** shops **are** quiet.

25.7 🔊
1 **There are some** shops.
2 **There are some** trees.
3 **There are lots of** cars.
4 **There are a few** churches.
5 **There are a few** flowers.
6 **There are some** cafés.
7 **There are a few** parks.

26

26.1 🔊
1 Fred works outside because **he's a farmer.**
2 Mick travels to Switzerland because **he goes skiing there.**
3 Saul goes to bed late because **he works in a restaurant.**
4 I get up at 5am because **I'm a mailman.**
5 Marion goes to the library because **she's a student.**
6 Colin works with children because **he's a teacher.**

26.2
1 he's a farmer
2 she's a teacher
3 he's a student
4 she goes to the gym
5 he's an actor
6 he has the flu
7 she's a chef

26.3 🔊
1 Aziz lives in the countryside because **he thinks it's beautiful.**
2 We don't have breakfast because **we're very busy.**
3 Mr. Aspinall gets up early because **he takes his dog for a walk.**
4 Arnold wears a suit because **he works in a bank.**
5 Vicky works outside because **she is a gardener.**
6 I work in a hospital because **I'm a doctor.**

26.4 🔊
1. Clara works in a theater because she is an actor.
2. Clara lives on a farm because she is a farmer.
3. Clara works in a hotel because she is a receptionist.
4. Mike lives on a farm because he is a farmer.
5. Mike works in a theater because he is an actor.
6. Mike works in a hotel because he is a receptionist.

27

27.1 🔊
1 kitchen
2 toilet
3 television
4 house
5 closet (US) / wardrobe (UK)
6 bathtub
7 garage
8 bedroom
9 apartment block (US) / block of flats (UK)
10 couch (US) / sofa (UK)
11 shower
12 dining room
13 door
14 window
15 table
16 chair
17 lamp
18 refrigerator (US) / fridge (UK)
19 study
20 bed
21 bookcase
22 bathroom
23 armchair

28

28.1 🔊
1 My friend **has** new glasses.
2 John **has** two dogs.
3 We **have** an old castle in our city.

4 They **have** a lot of parks in their town.
5 I **have** a beautiful necklace.
6 Alex **has** a new camera.
7 Our house **has** a lovely yard.
8 Phil and Sue **have** four daughters.
9 Pete **has** a new cell phone.
10 Your town **has** a big hotel.
11 I **have** a lot of friends.

28.2 🔊
1 Bob and Shirley **have** a big dog.
2 She **has** some new friends.
3 We **have** two sons at home.
4 James **has** two cars.
5 His house **has** three bedrooms.
6 Pam **has** lots of books at home.
7 He **has** two cats.
8 Sally's house **has** a new kitchen.
9 You **have** a beautiful house.
10 I **have** three sisters.
11 Kelly and Mark **have** a microwave.
12 We **have** a castle in our town.
13 Sanjay **has** a cat and a dog.
14 You **have** three brothers.
15 Ross **has** a new cell phone.
16 Our house **has** two bathrooms.
17 I **have** a couch in my room.
18 Washington **has** some lovely parks.

28.3 🔊
1 I have two sisters.
2 You have a beautiful house.
3 We have a garden.
4 Sam and Greg have a dog.
5 Marlon has a brother.
6 Fardale has an old castle.
7 They have a new car.

28.4
1 False
2 False
3 False
4 True
5 False
6 False
7 True

28.5 🔊
1 We don't have a computer at home.
2 My city doesn't have a castle.
3 Rob's house doesn't have a garage.
4 You don't have any sisters.
5 The village doesn't have any stores.

28.6 🔊
1. You have got a beautiful necklace.
2. She has not got any sisters.
3. We have not got a microwave.
4. Greg has not got a bike.
5. My town has got two theaters.
6. Chloe has not got a cat.
7. They have got a new house.

28.7
1. Our town
2. Adam and I
3. Sally and Jonathan
4. My friend Sam
5. Our house

28.8 🔊
1. I have a computer.
2. I have a sofa.
3. I have some tables.
4. We have a computer.
5. We have a sofa.
6. We have some tables.
7. He has a sofa.
8. He has a computer.
9. He has some tables.
10. He doesn't have a computer.
11. He doesn't have a sofa.

28.9
1. She has two bedrooms.
   She's got two bedrooms.
2. They have not got a dog.
   They haven't got a dog.
3. We have some chairs.
   We have got some chairs.
4. He has a brother.
   He's got a brother.
5. Carla has not got a sister.
   Carla hasn't got a sister.
6. You have a car.
   You've got a car.
7. Phil has a dog.
   Phil has got a dog.
8. You have got a yard.
   You've got a yard.
9. Jamal doesn't have a sofa.
   Jamal has not got a sofa.
10. They have a shower.
   They've got a shower.
11. May has a couch.
   May has got a couch.
12. He has not got a cat.
   He hasn't got a cat.

29

29.1 🔊
1. fork
2. washing machine
3. kettle
4. toaster
5. refrigerator
6. sink
7. plate

29.2 🔊
1. Does the house have a yard?
2. Does their kitchen have a refrigerator?
3. Does Bill's house have a big garage?
4. Do you have a sofa?
5. Does Barry have a kettle?
6. Does she have a barbecue at her house?
7. Does Marge have a new washing machine?
8. Do Jack and Marienne have a TV?
9. Does Leela's brother have a knife and fork?

29.3
1. Claudia
2. Paul
3. Jenny
4. Colin
5. Roberto

29.4 🔊
1. Yes, I do.
2. No, I don't.
3. Yes, I do.
4. Yes, I do.
5. No, I don't.

29.5 🔊
1. Do you have any chairs?
2. Do you have any knives?
3. Do you have a refrigerator?
4. Does he have any chairs?
5. Does he have any knives?
6. Does he have a refrigerator?
7. Do they have any chairs?
8. Do they have any knives?
9. Do they have a refrigerator?

29.6 🔊
1. Yes, **she does.**
2. Yes, **he does.**
3. No, **he doesn't.**
4. Yes, **it does.**
5. No, **they don't.**
6. No, **she doesn't.**
7. Yes, **he does.**

29.7 🔊
1. Have they got a microwave?
2. Have Shaun and Shania got a pet snake?
3. Has Charles got a camera?
4. Has Clarissa got a new laptop?
5. Has Carol's house got a big yard?
6. Have your friends got my book?
7. Has Brian got a new TV?

29.8 🔊
1. Has the kitchen got a microwave?
2. Has your house got a yard?
3. Have the Hendersons got a car?
4. Has Claire got my glasses?
5. Have your parents got a computer?
6. Has Paul got my book?
7. Has Brian got a magazine?
8. Have your neighbors got a basement?
9. Has your cell phone got a camera?
10. Has Sam got any money?
11. Has your town got a supermarket?
12. Has Brian got a sister?
13. Have your children got a cat?
14. Has your husband got a camera?
15. Has your school got a library?
16. Has Jane got a cell phone?
17. Have the kids got their bikes?

29.9 🔊
1. Have you got a refrigerator?
2. Have you got a car?
3. Have you got any brothers or sisters?
4. Has John got a refrigerator?
5. Has John got a car?
6. Has John got any brothers or sisters?
7. Has your kitchen got a refrigerator?

30

30.1 🔊
1. burger
2. spaghetti
3. juice
4. bread
5. fish

6 apple
7 eggs
8 drinks
9 banana
10 seafood
11 milk
12 strawberry
13 chocolate
14 cheese
15 orange
16 cereal
17 potatoes
18 sugar
19 butter
20 salad
21 meat
22 coffee
23 pasta
24 vegetables
25 cake
26 water
27 fruit
28 rice
29 breakfast
30 lunch
31 dinner

31

31.1 ◀))
COUNTABLE: **apple, burger, egg**
UNCOUNTABLE: **coffee, rice, juice**

31.2 ◀))
1 There **is** some orange juice.
2 Sam has **some** milk.
3 We have **some** salt.
4 There **are** some apples.
5 Rita has **a** banana.
6 I've got **some** eggs.

31.3 ◀))
1 four bananas
2 two eggs
3 some cheese
4 two burgers
5 one bar of chocolate

31.4
1 There is some salt.
   There isn't any salt.

2 Is there any wine?
   There isn't any wine.
3 There are some burgers.
   There aren't any burgers.
4 Are there any cookies?
   There aren't any cookies.
5 Are there any pastries?
   There are some pastries.
6 There is some bread.
   There isn't any bread.
7 Is there any rice?
   There isn't any rice
8 Is there any butter?
   There is some butter.
9 There are some pizzas.
   There aren't any pizzas.
10 Is there any cheese?
   There isn't any cheese.

31.5
1 False
2 True
3 False
4 True
5 False
6 True
7 True
8 False
9 False

31.6 ◀))
1 There's a **glass** of milk.
2 There are two **bags** of rice.
3 There's a **bar** of chocolate.
4 There's a **carton** of juice.
5 There are three **bottles** of water.
6 There's a **bowl** of pasta.
7 There are two **cups** of tea.

31.7 ◀))
1 There **is** a jar of coffee.
2 There **isn't** any rice.
3 There **are** two cartons of juice.
4 There **is** some meat.
5 There **are** two bottles of wine.
6 There **isn't** any bread.
7 There **is** a bag of flour.
8 There **is** some pasta.
9 There **are** two bars of chocolate.
10 There **isn't** any sugar.
11 There **is** some butter.

31.8
1 bowl
2 jar
3 bar
4 glass
5 carton
6 bag
7 cup
8 bottle
9 tube

31.9 ◀))
1 How **much** meat is there?
2 How **many** cartons of milk are there?
3 How **many** bowls of rice are there?
4 How **much** juice is there?
5 How **much** bread is there?
6 How **many** cups of tea are there?
7 How **many** bars of chocolate are there?
8 How **much** coffee is there?
9 How **many** jars of jam are there?
10 How **much** milk is there?
11 How **many** bags of flour are there?
12 How **much** pizza is there?
13 How **many** eggs are there?

31.10 ◀))
1. How many burgers are there?
2. How many eggs are there?
3. How many people are there?
4. How much rice is there?
5. How much water is there?
6. How much coffee is there?

32

32.1 ◀))
1 There are **too many** pears.
2 There is **too much** milk.
3 She has **too much** pasta.
4 We have **too many** bananas.
5 There is **too much** butter.
6 There are **too many** apples.
7 There are **too many** tomatoes.
8 I have **too much** juice.
9 There are **too many** mushrooms.
10 They have **too many** burgers.
11 Sue owns **too many** shoes.

32.2 🔊
1 There **are enough** pineapples.
2 There **are enough** mangoes.
3 There **is enough** sugar.
4 There **is enough** bread.
5 There **is enough** milk.
6 There **is enough** pasta.
7 There **are enough** apples.
8 There **are enough** oranges.
9 There **are enough** bananas.
10 There **is enough** chocolate.
11 There **are enough** eggs.
12 There **is enough** cheese.
13 There **are enough** tomatoes.
14 There **is enough** butter.
15 There **is enough** juice.

32.3
1 You have enough oranges.
  You have too many oranges.
2 There isn't enough sugar.
  There's too much sugar.
3 We don't have enough butter.
  We have enough butter.
4 There aren't enough eggs.
  There are too many eggs.
5 There is enough flour.
  There is too much flour.
6 There aren't enough potatoes.
  There are enough potatoes.
7 You don't have enough melons.
  You have too many melons.
8 He has enough bread.
  He has too much bread.
9 There isn't enough tea.
  There is enough tea.
10 We don't have enough milk.
  We have too much milk.
11 You have enough rice.
  You have too much rice.
12 There aren't enough mangoes.
  There are enough mangoes.
13 Martha doesn't have enough onions.
  Martha has too many onions.
14 You have enough carrots.
  You have too many carrots.

32.4
1 True
2 True
3 False
4 False
5 False

32.5 🔊
1 There are **not enough** carrots.
2 There are **enough** potatoes.
3 There are **not enough** tomatoes.
4 There is **not enough** pasta.
5 There is **too much** oil.
6 There is **enough** bread.
7 There is **enough** butter.
8 There is **too much** flour.
9 There is **not enough** sugar.
10 There are **enough** oranges.
11 There are **not enough** bananas.
12 There are **too many** eggs.
13 There is **enough** milk.

32.6 🔊
1 There **isn't** enough butter.
2 There **aren't** enough tomatoes.
3 There **aren't** enough mangoes.
4 You have too **many** bananas.
5 They don't have **enough** butter.
6 There **are** enough onions.
7 There **isn't** enough sugar.
8 You have **too** many pineapples.
9 They have too **much** bread.
10 You **don't** have enough apples.
11 They have **enough** flour.
12 There **are** too many potatoes.
13 There **is** too much salt.
14 There **is** too much chocolate.
15 There **are** too many mangoes.
16 You have **enough** eggs.
17 There **are** enough oranges.

32.7 🔊
1. There is enough butter.
2. There is not enough butter.
3. There is too much butter.
4. There are enough eggs.
5. There are not enough eggs.
6. There are too many eggs.
7. There is enough rice.
8. There is not enough rice.
9. There is too much rice.

33

33.1 🔊
1 gloves
2 hat

3 blue
4 boots
5 jeans
6 pink
7 red
8 suit
9 dress
10 belt
11 coat
12 green
13 skirt
14 shirt
15 black
16 scarf
17 yellow
18 sandals
19 socks
20 purple
21 extra small
22 small
23 medium
24 large
25 extra large
26 orange
27 shoes

34

34.1 🔊
1 That sweater **fits** you. It's the right size.
2 My mom always **chooses** my dad's clothes.
3 These jeans don't **fit**. They're too small.
4 I **own** 30 pairs of shoes.
5 I always **try on** clothes before I buy them.
6 Those shops **sell** very fashionable clothes.
7 We **buy** fruit at the market.
8 I **want** some shoes for my birthday.
9 I sometimes **pay** by credit card.

34.2 🔊
1 Ruth **does** a lot of her shopping on the internet.
2 The shop **doesn't** sell my size of clothes.
3 She **wears** short skirts.
4 Greg's jeans **don't** fit him.
5 Amy **owns** a lot of fashionable clothes.
6 We **pay** for our shopping with cash.
7 Duncan never **tries** on clothes before he buys them.

8 My parents usually **pay** for my clothes.

9 Peter **doesn't** own many clothes.

34.3 ◀))

1 That blouse **doesn't** fit you.

2 Sue always **tries** on her new clothes.

3 Rob **wants** a new tie for Christmas.

4 Peter **buys** his meat at the butcher's shop.

5 Jose **owns** a beautiful house in France.

6 My jeans **don't** fit me. They're too big.

7 Samantha **chooses** high-quality clothes.

8 They **sell** vegetables in the market.

9 Do you **want** a new shirt for your birthday?

34.4 ◀))

1 This is a **new** T-shirt.

2 These are **short** jeans.

3 This is an **expensive** tie.

4 This is a **large** sweater.

5 This is a **blue** dress.

6 This is an **old** T-shirt.

7 These are **cheap** shoes.

8 This is a **short** skirt.

9 This is a **red** shirt.

10 These are **big** shoes.

11 This is a **small** sweater.

34.5

1 a red skirt

2 a red scarf

3 brown shoes

4 blue jeans

5 green coat.

34.6

1 cheap

2 short

3 long

4 hard

5 soft

34.7 ◀))

1 too hard

2 too old

3 too expensive

4 too long

5 too soft

6 too short

34.8 ◀))

1 Claire's hat is **too small**.

2 These shoes are **too expensive**.

3 Sophie's pullover is **too small**.

4 Corrine's coat is **big enough**.

5 Emma's sweater is **too big**.

6 Chloe's scarf is **too long**.

7 Phoebe's shoes are **too big**.

8 Joshua's jacket is **too small**.

35

35.1

1 False **2** True **3** True **4** True **5** False

6 True **7** False **8** True **9** False

35.2 ◀))

1 Our house has a pretty little yard.

2 James has an ugly leather jacket.

3 Pete has an old wooden table.

4 This is a brilliant new book.

5 Shelley's got a beautiful glass bottle.

6 That was such a boring old film.

7 That's an ugly woolen sweater.

8 Those are boring black shoes.

9 I've got a horrible old car.

10 Simone has a beautiful gray parrot.

11 That's a horrible old house!

12 You've got a nice red shirt.

35.3 ◀))

1 Jill's got a beautiful black dog.

2 Simon has a nice new house.

3 They have an ugly old car.

4 Those are pretty red shoes.

5 That's an ugly pink hat.

6 Greg has a horrible brown snake.

7 You've got a beautiful black bag.

8 This is a great new book.

35.4

1 metal

2 paper

3 wool

4 glass

5 leather

6 wood

35.5

1 plastic **2** wooden **3** glass

4 leather **5** plastic **6** wool

7 wooden **8** paper **9** wool

10 plastic **11** leather **12** metal **13** metal

35.6 ◀))

1 Four **plastic** cups.

2 An ugly **wooden** table.

3 An old **leather** jacket.

4 Three **metal** chairs.

5 A green **wool** sweater.

6 A brown **paper** bag.

7 Beautiful **fabric**.

36

36.1 ◀))

1 roller-skating

2 rugby

3 golf

4 snowboarding

5 cycling

6 badminton

7 ice hockey

8 baseball

9 skateboarding

10 swimming

11 running

12 basketball

13 tennis

14 skiing

15 horse riding

36.2 ◀))

1 baseball bat

2 golf course

3 snowboard

4 swimming pool

5 golf club

6 running track

7 skateboard

8 stadium

9 surfboard

10 tennis court

11 skis

37

37.1 ◀))

1 Douglas **goes cycling** with his brother on Sundays.

2 Phil and John **go skating** in the winter.

3 Mr. Henderson **goes sailing** in the Mediterranean in the summer.

4 Veronica **goes dancing** with her friends on the weekend.

5 They **go hiking** in the mountains in Scotland.

6 Lawrence **goes swimming** on Tuesdays.

7 Ted **goes skateboarding** on Saturday morning.

8 I **go horseback riding** in France each year.

9 She **goes shopping** in Milan at Christmas.

10 We **go fishing** after work on Mondays.

11 Anne **goes surfing** in California.

37.2 ◀))

1 Jane goes **dancing** on Friday nights.

2 Our dad goes **sailing** in the summer.

3 I go **fishing** in the evening.

4 Do you go **running** in the morning?

5 They go **cycling** in the summer.

6 Sam goes **swimming** on Sundays.

7 I go **horseback riding** daily.

8 Claire goes **shopping** in London.

9 Omar goes **skateboarding** daily.

10 Do you go **dancing** with her?

11 Rachel goes **hiking** in Peru.

12 I go **snowboarding** in the winter.

13 Bob and Steve go **surfing** in Tahiti.

37.3 ◀))

1 snowboarding

2 running

3 fishing

4 swimming

5 skateboarding

6 dancing

7 surfing

8 shopping

9 cycling

10 sailing

11 riding

37.4 ◀))

1 I **go** shopping in the evening.

2 Jan **goes** skateboarding on Fridays.

3 Pete **goes** sailing on the weekend.

4 Sam **goes** skating every December.

5 I **go** running on Wednesday.

6 They **go** fishing with their friends.

7 Sarah **goes** dancing on Saturdays.

37.5 ◀))

1 Do you **play** chess?

2 Paolo **plays** badminton at the weekend.

3 My father **plays** golf with his friends.

4 We **don't play** baseball anymore.

5 I **play** tennis with my brother.

6 Greg **doesn't play** basketball.

7 Liz **plays** racquet ball on the weekend.

8 Your dad **doesn't play** soccer.

9 Our dog **plays** with its ball.

10 Mike **plays** soccer on Saturdays.

11 We **don't play** golf in the winter.

12 Pammy **doesn't play** tennis.

37.6 ◀))

1 Does he play badminton on Fridays?

2 Does Noah play golf with his grandpa?

3 Do they play basketball with their friends?

4 Does Georgia play baseball at school?

5 Do we play tennis in the summer?

6 Do Tim's parents play chess in the evening?

37.7

1 False **2** True **3** False **4** True
5 False **6** True **7** True

37.8 ◀))

1 John **plays** badminton on Wednesday.

2 You **go** fishing with your brother.

3 My uncle **plays** chess with my aunt.

4 We **go** dancing in the evening.

5 Sally's dad **plays** rugby.

6 Bartou **goes** cycling in the mountains.

7 Ramona **plays** racquet ball with her dad.

8 Our kids **play** baseball after school.

9 Simon and Pam **go** surfing in the summer.

10 They **play** basketball every Saturday.

11 We **go** snowboarding in Austria.

37.9 ◀))

1 I **play baseball** with my friends at school.

2 Anna **goes skateboarding** in the afternoon on Sundays.

3 Mrs. Amir **plays chess** with her husband in the evening.

4 Max **plays badminton** on Tuesdays and Fridays.

5 Peter **goes fishing** with his brother on Mondays and Wednesdays.

38

38.1 ◀))

1 play a musical instrument

2 write

3 do yoga

4 play video games

5 watch television

6 walk / hike

7 go the gym

8 sew

9 go shopping

10 do the gardening

11 draw

12 go camping

13 bake

14 listen to music

15 do puzzles

16 watch a movie

17 visit a museum

18 play cards

19 see a play

20 meet friends

21 knit

22 paint

23 read

24 go bird watching

25 go out for a meal

26 play chess

27 take photos

39

39.1

1 True **2** False **3** False **4** False
5 True **6** False **7** True

39.2 ◀))

1 They sometimes go to the theater.

2 Mike never goes running after work.

3 You always go to bed early.

4 Jane often goes shopping on Saturday.

5 We usually eat dinner at 6pm.

39.3

1 never **2** sometimes **3** often
4 usually **5** always **6** often

39.4 ◀))

1 Clara **never** plays chess with her grandfather.

2 Enzo **always** eats chocolate ice cream.

3 Paul **sometimes** goes fishing in the morning.

4 My parents **usually** drive to work.

5 Gill **never** goes shopping with her mom.

6 You **sometimes** go to the gym in the town.

7 Shelley **usually** watches TV in the evening.

8 My dog **always** sleeps under the table.

9 We **sometimes** play baseball in the summer.

10 Tim **usually** rides his horse on the weekend.

39.5 ◀))

1 How often does Steph watch TV?
2 How often do you visit your dad?
3 When do they play soccer?
4 When do you usually go to bed?
5 How often does May go running?
6 How often do you play tennis?
7 How often does Jo read a book?

39.6 ◀))

1 **She goes to the gym** on Wednesdays.
2 **He plays soccer** in the evening.
3 She never **goes to the theater**.
4 He sometimes **reads a newspaper**.
5 **She visits her family** four times a year.
6 **He plays baseball** every afternoon.
7 **She goes shopping** twice a week.
8 **I read** a book every evening.
9 She sometimes **makes a cake**.

39.7 ◀))

1 How often does Jimmy play soccer?
2 How often do you phone your grandma?
3 How often does Sheila get up at 7am?
4 How often do you read a book?
5 How often does Sally go to work?
6 How often do you play badminton?
7 How often does your daughter go running?
8 How often does Megan go fishing?
9 How often do you watch TV?

39.8 ◀))

1 She always **goes** dancing on the weekend.
2 I often **go** fishing.
3 My mom never **gets up** early.
4 Seb usually **plays** soccer on weekends.
5 Tracy never **watches** TV in the evening.
6 We sometimes **take** the bus to work.
7 Doug often **plays** tennis on Fridays.

40

40.1 ◀))

1 We like cake.
2 I hate tennis.
3 We love basketball.
4 Shelley loves pizza.
5 They hate board games.
6 I don't like pasta.
7 Samantha likes chocolate.

40.2

1 salad 2 sports 3 playing tennis 4 golf
5 listening to music 6 classical music
7 going shopping 8 going to the cinema
9 scary films 10 taking photos

40.3 ◀))

1 Chris doesn't like spiders.
2 They hate Paris.
3 Mrs. McGregor doesn't like cats.
4 We hate soccer.
5 We don't like wine.
6 Simone hates her horse.
7 He doesn't like your necklace.
8 Jean-Marie hates sports.
9 Colin doesn't like pizza.
10 Douglas doesn't like Anne.
11 Cynthia loves dogs.
12 We hate chocolate.
13 You don't like cheese.
14 Susan doesn't like pizza.

40.4 ◀))

1. They love cats.
2. They love running.
3. They love pizza.
4. They love snakes.
5. Arnold hates cats.
6. Arnold hates running.
7. Arnold hates pizza.
8. Arnold hates snakes.
9. My mother hates cats.
10. My mother hates running.
11. My mother hates pizza.
12. My mother hates snakes.

40.5

1 She likes cooking.
2 Her favorite is Italian food.
3 She doesn't like cooking meat.
4 She cooks for her friends and family.

5 She doesn't like fast food.
6 She hates candy.

40.6 ◀))

1 I **hate** cities, but I **love** the country.
2 Archie **likes** ice cream, and he **loves** pizza.
3 He **loves** meat, but he **hates** fish.
4 Francis **doesn't like** coffee, but he **likes** tea.
5 We **hate** Mondays, but we **love** Fridays.
6 My dad **dislikes** classical music, but he **loves** rock.

40.7 ◀))

1 Sam likes watching soccer **because it's exciting.**
2 Marie loves pizza. **She thinks it's delicious.**
3 I love reading history books **because they're really interesting.**
4 Sally doesn't like running **because it is tiring.**
5 Peggy does not like eating meat **because she is a vegetarian.**
6 Paolo does not eat chocolate **because he doesn't have a sweet tooth.**
7 Jemma hates snakes. **She thinks they are scary.**

40.8

1 hot
2 interesting
3 delicious
4 boring
5 tiring

41

41.1 ◀))

1 sing a song
2 dance
3 electric guitar
4 headphones
5 opera
6 keyboard
7 piano
8 rap
9 country
10 album
11 rock

12 guitar
13 Latin
14 orchestra
15 jazz
16 flute
17 conductor
18 saxophone
19 audience
20 guitar player
21 play the trumpet
22 trumpet
23 concert
24 violin
25 drum
26 microphone
27 harmonica

42

42.1 🔊
1 Nick's favorite uncle is an actor.
2 Jo's favorite book is *Puzzling People*.
3 Jay's favorite instrument is the piano.
4 Paul's favorite drink is orange juice.
5 Blake's favorite animal is the tiger.
6 Dan's favorite place is his garden.
7 Sanjay's favorite season is winter.
8 Max's favorite hobby is painting.
9 Greg's favorite food is rice.
10 Levi's favorite sport is baseball.
11 Martha's favorite country is France.
12 Simone's favorite lesson is science.
13 Maya's favorite dessert is cake.
14 Karina's favorite fruit is pineapple.
15 Their favorite city is London.
16 Kate's favorite pet is her parrot.
17 Zoe's favorite pastime is dancing.

42.2
1 math
2 Friday
3 red
4 chocolate cake
5 baseball
6 fall

42.3 🔊
1 Barbara likes listening to music in the evening.
2 Arnold's favorite food is ice cream and pizza.

3 Craig doesn't like getting up in the morning.
4 Seb's favorite type of music is hip-hop.
5 Ruth likes orange juice.
6 Daniel's favorite animal is the lion.
7 I like bacon and eggs for breakfast.
8 Aziz doesn't like lasagna or spaghetti.
9 Miguel loves going to the movie theater.

42.4
1 True 2 False 3 False 4 False
5 True 6 False 7 False 8 True 9 True
10 True

42.5 🔊
1 Arnie's favorite sport is **tennis**.
2 Joan's favorite animal is a **dolphin**.
3 Hassan's favorite actor is **Chris Minota**.
4 Pam's favorite number is **21**.
5 Jane's favorite sport is **badminton**.
6 Dora's favorite ice cream is **strawberry**.
7 Jim's favorite food is **spaghetti**.

42.6 🔊
1. She loves salsa dancing.
2. She loves sailing.
3. She loves chocolate ice cream.
4. Simon loves salsa dancing.
5. Simon loves sailing.
6. Simon loves chocolate ice cream.
7. She likes salsa dancing.
8. She likes sailing.
9. She likes chocolate ice cream.
10. Simon likes salsa dancing.
11. Simon likes sailing.
12. Simon likes chocolate ice cream.
13. Her favorite food is chocolate ice cream.
14. Her favorite sport is sailing.

43

43.1 🔊
1 talk
2 shout
3 throw
4 listen
5 lift
6 hit
7 walk
8 add
9 kick

10 make (a snowman)
11 carry
12 fly
13 sit
14 act
15 see
16 do (homework)
17 ride
18 catch
19 spell
20 move
21 stand up
22 understand
23 jump
24 climb
25 subtract
26 drive
27 work

44

44.1
1 I can ride a horse.
  I can't ride a horse.
2 I cannot climb a tree.
  I can't climb a tree.
3 I can speak French.
  I cannot speak French.
4 I can sing.
  I can't sing.
5 I can lift a box.
  I cannot lift a box.
6 I can fly a kite.
  I can't fly a kite.
7 I cannot catch a fish.
  I can't catch a fish.
8 I can swim.
  I can't swim.

44.2 🔊
1 Kate **can hit** the ball.
2 Paul **can't do** math.
3 Helen **can spell** very well.
4 Ivan **can't run** very fast.
5 Sara **can move** the chair.
6 Alex **can't play** badminton.
7 Lynn **can ride** a bicycle.

44.3 🔊
1 Eliza cannot drive a car.
2 Jonathan can play the piano.

3 Cathy can't jump very high.
4 Mick can throw a stick.
5 Laura can't do math.
6 Alan can lift the box.
7 Julia can't swim very far.

44.4
1 Can **2** Can't **3** Can't **4** Can **5** Can

44.5 🔊
1 Can Maria and Juan spell English words?
2 Can the children do their math homework?
3 Can you sing difficult jazz songs?
4 Can Mark ride a horse?
5 Can Jack climb a tree?
6 Can he carry that box?
7 Can Carlos kick a football?
8 Can Adam and Ella dance the tango?
9 Can Peter and John swim?

44.6 🔊
1 Jack is a diving teacher. He can **swim very well**.
2 Carla lives on a farm. She can **ride a horse** and look after animals.
3 Bobby is good at languages. He can **speak Russian**.
4 Nuna likes going on winter vacations. She can **ski well**.
5 Jim is a great children's teacher. He can **tell stories** well.

44.7 🔊
1 Yes, **I can**. **2** No, **I can't**. **3** Yes, **I can**.
4 No, **I can't**. **5** No, **I can't**. **6** Yes, **I can**.
7 No, **I can't**. **8** No, **I can't**. **9** No, **I can't**.
10 Yes, **I can**. **11** Yes, **I can**.

44.8 🔊
1. I can ride a bicycle.
2. I can't ride a bicycle.
3. She can ride a bicycle.
4. She can't ride a bicycle.
5. They can ride a bicycle.
6. They can't ride a bicycle.
7. I can swim a mile.
8. I can't swim a mile.
9. She can swim a mile
10. She can't swim a mile.
11. They can swim a mile
12. They can't swim a mile.
13. I can play tennis.
14. I can't play tennis.
15. She can play tennis.
16. She can't play tennis.
17. They can play tennis.
18. They can't play tennis.

45

45.1 🔊
1 My friend speaks too **quietly**.
2 A turtle walks very **slowly**.
3 Alan can speak German **well**.
4 My dog can run very **fast**.
5 I get up very **early**.

45.2
1 Patrick is good at dancing.
2 Caitlin bakes well.
3 My mother is good at writing.
4 Ethan plays the guitar well.
5 Aimee is good at skiing.
6 They swim well.
7 We are good at speaking English.
8 Lara climbs trees well.

45.3 🔊
1 Haruda sometimes arrives **late** for school.
2 My cousin Paul runs **quickly**.
3 Shelley sings **beautifully**.
4 Our neighbors talk so **noisily** at night.
5 Rosa reads very **slowly**.
6 I can pass this exam **easily**.
7 My aunt drives very **carefully**.
8 Anita works very **hard**.
9 We **usually** go to bed at 11pm.
10 Angela speaks English **badly**.
11 A cheetah runs very **fast**.
12 Sarah eats her food very **quickly**.
13 Andrew does his homework **well**.

45.4 🔊
1. I am good at drawing.
2. I am good at playing the drums.
3. I am good at English.
4. I am bad at drawing.
5. I am bad at playing the drums.
6. I am bad at English.
7. Jennifer is good at drawing.
8. Jennifer is good at playing the drums.
9. Jennifer is good at English.
10. Jennifer is bad at drawing.
11. Jennifer is bad at playing the drums.
12. Jennifer is bad at English.
13. We are good at drawing.
14. We are good at playing the drums.
15. We are good at English.
16. We are bad at drawing.
17. We are bad at playing the drums.
18. We are bad at English.

46

46.1 🔊
1 Pedro is really good at history.
2 You speak French really well.
3 Sandra is very good at singing.
4 Sal is quite good at skiing.
5 Your uncle can swim very well.
6 They can run quite fast.
7 Mr. Henderson is really good at golf.

46.2 🔊
1 Arnold isn't very good at art and design.
2 My cousin is really good at speaking English.
3 Jean is quite good at climbing mountains.

46.3
1 My aunt is quite good at speaking Polish.
2 Your brother surfs really well.
3 Katie paints very well.
4 Silvia is really good at singing.
5 Martina is very good at dancing.
6 Serge cooks quite well.
7 Sonia is really good at playing chess.
8 Ricky runs very well.
9 Peter is quite good at drawing.
10 My mom speaks Greek really well.
11 David is very good at playing the drums.

46.4 🔊
1 Charlotte can ski quite well.
2 Harry sings really quietly.
3 My aunt walks very slowly.
4 Elizabeth speaks Russian very well.
5 My dog can jump quite high.
6 William speaks Japanese really badly.
7 Philip eats quite noisily.

47.1
1. She wants to have a cat.
   She'd like to have a cat.
2. They would like to visit Tokyo.
   They'd like to visit Tokyo.
3. I want to eat an orange.
   I would like to eat an orange.
4. You want to learn Spanish.
   You'd like to learn Spanish.
5. We want to go to a café.
   We would like to go to a café.
6. He would like to live in Germany.
   He'd like to live in Germany.
7. We want to swim in a lake.
   We'd like to swim in a lake.

47.2 ◀))
1. They'd like to go sailing on a sailboat.
2. Dan would like to travel to New York.
3. Sharon wants to read her book.
4. Doug would like to climb a mountain.
5. We want to go on vacation to Tahiti.

47.3 ◀))
1. Douglas wants to have pasta.
2. They'd like to go home tomorrow.
3. Does Chris want to go swimming later?
4. Sheila doesn't want to see Paul.
5. Would you like to visit us tomorrow?
6. Our children want to go to college.
7. She'd like to buy a new cell phone.
8. Jenny wants to go shopping on Friday.
9. Simon would like to be a doctor.
10. I would like to have a hamburger.
11. Would you like to be a vet?
12. Chloe doesn't want to eat that pizza.
13. Do you want to read this book?
14. They would like to watch TV.
15. She wants to go to the party.

47.4 ◀))
1. I'd like to drive around America.
2. I'd like to travel around America.
3. We want to drive around America.
4. We want to travel around America.
5. Greg wants to drive around America.
6. Greg wants to travel around America.
7. I'd like to drive to Miami.
8. I'd like to travel to Miami.
9. We want to drive to Miami.
10. We want to travel to Miami.
11. Greg wants to drive to Miami.
12. Greg wants to travel to Miami.

47.5
1. Yes, he would.
2. No, he doesn't.
3. Yes, he would.
4. Yes, she does.
5. No, she doesn't.
6. No, he doesn't.
7. Yes, she does.

47.6 ◀))
1. Marie wants to go snowboarding in Austria.
2. Mario doesn't want to go to school today.
3. She wants to climb that mountain.
4. Tony would like to play golf in Scotland.

47.7 ◀))
1. Do you want **to** go home now?
2. Claude would **like** to learn French.
3. He would **like** to go swimming.
4. Paolo wants **to** get a new cat.
5. Would you like **to** visit China?
6. **He'd** like to go to work later today.
7. Peter **wants** to go to college next year.
8. They **don't** want to go to school today.
9. My sister **wants** to go to Greece this summer.

47.8 ◀))
1. Would Peter like to go fishing?
2. Does Marion want to play tennis on Saturday?
3. Would he like to visit India?
4. Would Mr. Evans like to play chess tonight?
5. Would you like to play squash this evening?
6. Does Sam want to go to the park again?
7. Would they like to travel around China?

48.1 ◀))
1. My mother would really like to travel to Spain.
2. Doug would quite like to learn French.
3. Sally would quite like to do an art degree.
4. Don's brother would like to practice the piano.
5. I'd really like to go to a rock concert tonight.
6. Martha would like to study chemistry in college.
7. My kids would quite like to study German at school.

48.2 ◀))
1. Edith would really like to read her new book.
2. They'd really like to go to a concert.
3. I'd really like to go to France on vacation.
4. Jean-Paul would quite like to speak to you.
5. We'd quite like to eat pizza tonight.
6. Jeremy would really like to play his piano.
7. They'd really like to pass their chemistry exam.
8. Sophie would quite like to speak Mandarin.
9. David would really like to visit his son.

48.3 ◀))
1. I'd really like to improve my English.
2. I'd really like to learn Japanese.
3. I'd really like to do a history degree.
4. I'd quite like to improve my English.
5. I'd quite like to learn Japanese.
6. I'd quite like to do a history degree.
7. Sam would really like to learn Japanese.
8. Sam would really like to do a history degree.
9. Sam would quite like to learn Japanese.
10. Sam would quite like to do a history degree.
11. We'd really like to learn Japanese.
12. We'd really like to do a history degree.
13. We'd quite like to learn Japanese.
14. We'd quite like to do a history degree.

48.4
1. history
2. review
3. music
4. study
5. drama
6. math
7. degree
8. exams

48.5 ◀))
1. Phillipa goes to **college**.
2. Rome is **a beautiful city**.
3. We are at **home** at the moment.

④ Sharon goes to **school** at 9am.
⑤ **The college** is far away.
⑥ Peter goes **to bed** at 10pm.
⑦ My uncle is at **the mosque** today.
⑧ Jim goes to **church** on Sundays.
⑨ Sean leaves **home** at 7:30am.
⑩ Seb lives next to **the hospital**.

48.6 🔊

① Carol leaves work at 6pm every day.
② Jane can drive you to school tomorrow.
③ Chris lives across from the hospital.
④ Carl is at home at the moment.
⑤ Julia has a beautiful horse.
⑥ The hospital isn't very far.
⑦ We go to bed at 11pm usually.
⑧ Ottersley is a beautiful town.
⑨ Your shoes are under the bed.

48.7 🔊

① Sally is **in hospital**. She is ill.
② York is **a** pretty town.
③ She is **at home** now.
④ Lizzie goes **to church** on Sundays.
⑤ Bob is **at work** at the moment.
⑥ Christopher has **a** new car.
⑦ Jim goes **to bed** early on Sundays.
⑧ Carlos is **a** very talented boy.
⑨ Sarah and John are **a** great team.
⑩ Mary **bought three** new pens.
⑪ He jumped into **the** water and started swimming.
⑫ New York is **a** beautiful city.
⑬ **The** children were playing in the sun.
⑭ I can't **play soccer** on Monday.
⑮ Can you play **the** classical guitar?

48.8

① Sarah
② Eddie
③ Robert
④ Oliver

Acknowledgments

The publisher would like to thank:
Jo Kent, Trish Burrow, and Emma Watkins for additional text; Thomas Booth, Helen Fanthorpe, Helen Leech, Carrie Lewis, and Vicky Richards for editorial assistance; Stephen Bere, Sarah Hilder, Amy Child, Fiona Macdonald, and Simon Murrell for additional design work; Simon Mumford for maps and national flags; Peter Chrisp for fact checking; Penny Hands, Amanda Learmonth, and Carrie Lewis for proofreading; Elizabeth Wise for indexing; Tatiana Boyko, Rory Farrell, Clare Joyce, and Viola Wang for additional illustrations; Liz Hammond for editing audio scripts and managing audio recordings; Hannah Bowen and Scarlett O'Hara for compiling audio scripts; Jordan Killiard for mixing and mastering audio recordings; Heather Hughes, Tommy Callan, Tom Morse, Gillian Reid, and Sonia Charbonnier for creative technical support; Priyanka Kharbanda, Suefa Lee, Shramana Purkayastha, Isha Sharma, Sheryl Sadana for editorial support; Yashashvi Choudhary, Jaileen Kaur, Bhavika Mathur, Richa Verma, Anita Yadav, Apurva Agarwal for design support; Deepak Negi and Nishwan Rasool for picture research; Rohan Sinha for managerial and moral support.

All images are copyright DK.
For more information, please visit **www.dk.com/uk/information/contact-us.**